AFRICAN AMERICAN LITERATURE

GLOBE FEARON
EDUCATIONAL PUBLISHER

Paramount Publishing

Executive Editor: Virginia Seeley

Senior Editor: Barbara Levadi

Project Editor: Karen Hill

Contributing Editor: Jerrie Cobb Scott, Ph.D.
Central State University
Wilberforce, Ohio

Editorial Developer: Brown Publishing Network, Inc.

Production Editor: June E. Bodansky

Art Director: Nancy Sharkey

Production Manager: Penny Gibson

Production Coordinator: Walter Niedner

Desktop Specialist: José A. López

Marketing Managers: Sandra Hutchison and Elmer Ildefonso

Cover Design: Richard Puder Design

Photo Research: Omni Photo Communications, Inc.

Cover: My Mother's Work. design by Roland L. Freeman.
Poetry by Ja A. Jahannes.

Literature and art acknowledgments can be found on pages 152–154.

Printed in the United States of America.
2 3 4 5 6 7 8 9 10   97 96 95

ISBN: 0-835-90610-8

GLOBE FEARON
EDUCATIONAL PUBLISHER
PARAMUS, NEW JERSEY

Paramount Publishing

CONTENTS

UNIT 1: NONFICTION   2

My Dungeon Shook   4
    by James Baldwin
      A letter from *The Fire Next Time*

The Long Shadow of Little Rock   12
    by Elizabeth Eckford as told to Daisy Bates
      An autobiographical account from
      The Long Shadow of Little Rock

Waiting for Malcolm   18
    by Ja A. Jahannes
      An excerpt from the essay
      "Waiting for Malcolm"

Sweet Summer   27
    by Bebe Moore Campbell
      An excerpt from the novel
      Sweet Summer

Focus on Writing   38

UNIT 2: FICTION   40

The Boy Who Painted Christ Black   42
    by John Henrik Clarke
      A short story

Raymond's Run   52
    by Toni Cade Bambara
      A short story from *Gorilla, My Love*

Roll of Thunder, Hear My Cry   65
    by Mildred D. Taylor
      An excerpt from the novel
      Roll of Thunder, Hear My Cry

This Strange New Feeling   74
    by Julius Lester
      An excerpt from the novel
      This Strange New Feeling

Focus on Writing   84

UNIT 3: POETRY 86

Section 1: Toward Tomorrow's Triumphs 88

Nikki-Rosa 89
by Nikki Giovanni

listen children 91
by Lucille Clifton

Another Mountain 92
by Abiodun Oyewole

On the Pulse of Morning 93
by Maya Angelou

Section 2: In Our World 98

#4 99
by Doughtry Long

Knoxville, Tennessee 100
by Nikki Giovanni

Ka 'Ba 101
by Amiri Baraka

Who Can Be Born Black 102
by Mari Evans

Focus on Writing 104

UNIT 4: DRAMA 106

Escape to Freedom 108
by Ossie Davis
An excerpt from the play
Escape to Freedom

Focus on Writing 150

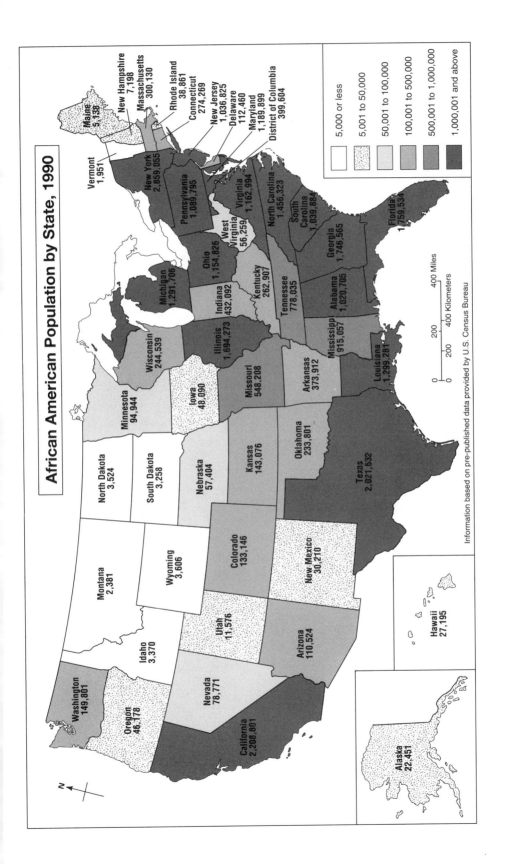

African American Population by State, 1990

Legend:
- 5,000 or less
- 5,001 to 50,000
- 50,001 to 100,000
- 100,001 to 500,000
- 500,001 to 1,000,000
- 1,000,001 and above

Maine 5,138
New Hampshire 7,198
Massachusetts 300,130
Rhode Island 38,861
Connecticut 274,269
New Jersey 1,036,825
Delaware 112,460
Maryland 1,189,899
District of Columbia 399,604
Vermont 1,951
New York 2,859,055
Pennsylvania 1,089,795
Virginia 1,162,994
West Virginia 56,259
North Carolina 1,456,323
South Carolina 1,039,884
Georgia 1,746,565
Florida 1,759,534
Ohio 1,154,826
Kentucky 262,907
Tennessee 778,035
Alabama 1,020,705
Michigan 1,291,706
Indiana 432,092
Illinois 1,694,273
Mississippi 915,057
Louisiana 1,299,281
Wisconsin 244,539
Missouri 548,208
Arkansas 373,912
Minnesota 94,944
Iowa 48,090
Kansas 143,076
Oklahoma 233,801
Texas 2,021,632
North Dakota 3,524
South Dakota 3,258
Nebraska 57,404
Colorado 133,146
New Mexico 30,210
Montana 2,381
Wyoming 3,606
Utah 11,576
Arizona 110,524
Idaho 3,370
Nevada 78,771
Washington 149,801
Oregon 46,178
California 2,208,801
Hawaii 27,195
Alaska 22,451

400 Miles
400 Kilometers
0 200
0 200

Information based on pre-published data provided by U.S. Census Bureau.

Titles of literature are placed in the time box to reflect, when possible, the historical time or event about which the selections are written.

Escape to Freedom ▼
1830s Abolitionist movement gains force.
1831 Nat Turner leads the most famous slave rebellion in U.S. history.

This Strange New Feeling ▼
1850 Compromise of 1850 strengthens Fugitive Slave Law.
1861-1865 Civil War ends African American slavery.

Roll of Thunder, Hear My Cry ▼
The Boy Who Painted Christ Black ▼
1920s Harlem Renaissance produces many African American artists.
1929 The Great Depression begins: the stock market crashes, banks fail, and millions lose their jobs.
1938 U.S. Supreme Court says states must provide equal schools for African Americans.

Nikki-Rosa ▼
Knoxville, Tennessee ▼
#4 ▼
1941-1945 United States enters World War II. Armed forces are still segregated. Many African Americans earn medals for distinguished service.

The Long Shadow of Little Rock ▼
1954 U.S. Supreme Court declares segregation in public schools unconstitutional in the landmark case *Brown* v. *Board of Education.*
1955 Civil Rights Movement begins: Rosa Parks is arrested in Montgomery, Alabama, for refusing to give up her bus seat to a white passenger. Martin Luther King, Jr., urges bus boycott that lasts one year.

My Dungeon Shook ▼
Waiting for Malcolm ▼
Sweet Summer ▼
1960 Four African American college students begin sit-in protest movement at lunch counter in North Carolina.
1963 100th anniversary of Emancipation Proclamation.

Ka 'Ba ▼
1965 Malcolm X is assassinated in New York City.
1966 Black Panther Party founded.
1968 Martin Luther King, Jr., is assassinated in Memphis, Tennessee, sparking urban riots. Record number of African American representatives is elected to Congress.

Raymond's Run ▼
Listen Children ▼
1971 NAACP reports worst unemployment for African Americans since 1930s.

Another Mountain ▼
1979 U. S. Supreme Court approves affirmative action programs to encourage employment for people of color.

Who Can Be Born Black ▼
1980s Number of African American elected officials increases greatly, five times the number in 1970.
1983 Federal holiday established to honor Martin Luther King, Jr.

On the Pulse of Morning ▼
1992 Jury acquits Los Angeles policemen accused of beating African American man, Rodney King, triggering riots and protests in the city.
1992 William Clinton elected President of the United States; captures 80 percent of the African American vote.

DEAR STUDENT:

All the cultures that make up the United States have played a major part in molding the history of this country. In the following pages, you will read literature written by African Americans. As you read the letter, autobiographical accounts, stories, poems, and the play, reflect on the special values and heritage that are part of the African American experience.

The literature in this book is arranged into four units. Each unit represents a particular form of literature. The selections in the first unit are factual in nature and focus on personal experiences. The second unit consists of three fictional stories that explore growing up as an African American and one story that explores the relationship between a slave and a planter. The third unit presents two groups of poems. In the first group, the poets explore the strengths they draw from their heritage as African Americans. In the second group, the poets offer rich images of their African American families and communities. The fourth unit presents a drama about the youth of a famous African American.

The page following the table of contents features a map that shows the African American population throughout the United States. A time box displays information about historical events that occurred during the period in which each selection is set.

As you read, think about the writing. The selections represent the experiences of many who have struggled to recapture a distinct, rich cultural identity. The literature of African Americans reveals a deep pride in their ancient heritage and a belief in the survival of their culture.

UNIT 1

NONFICTION OF THE AFRICAN AMERICANS

Unlike fiction, which describes imaginary characters and events, nonfiction features real people, real places, and events that actually happened.

You are surrounded by nonfiction in a great variety of forms, and it probably accounts for much of the reading you do in and out of school. Nonfiction such as textbooks and newspaper and magazine articles generally provides current, factual information about the world. There are other forms of nonfiction, however, that offer something else—an author's interpretation of people and events that exist in the real world. Such nonfiction includes essays, letters, autobiographies, editorials, journals, interviews, and speeches.

The selections in this unit were written about events that took place in the late 1950s and early 1960s, when there was a surge in the expectations, hopes, and frustrations of African Americans. In the first, an impassioned letter, James Baldwin urges his nephew to help bring about social change in the United States. In the second selection, an autobiographical sketch, Ja A. Jahannes recalls the personal impact of a speech made by Malcolm X. The third is Elizabeth Eckford's account of her role in the news-making integration of an Arkansas high school. In the last piece, Bebe Moore Campbell recalls her experience as one of the few African American students in her school. As you read these selections, think about how the authors use their personal perspectives to help the reader respond to real events.

This realistic painting, *Short Stories*, portrays an outdoor gathering of students and a reader, with one child peeking out—perhaps inviting the viewer to join the group. The popular African American artist Joseph Holston has produced two decades of recognized work. His paintings and prints are exhibited widely in museums. They are also found in the private collections of well-known African American entertainers and political leaders.

INTRODUCTION

My Dungeon Shook

James Baldwin was born in Harlem, New York City, in 1924, the son of a minister. Baldwin briefly became a Pentecostal minister when he was still a teen, but his real talent during those years was as a writer. In high school he became editor of the school's literary magazine. After graduation, while working at several odd jobs, he wrote articles about racial issues that were published in several well-known journals. Then, at the age of 24, he received a grant to study in France. During a ten-year stay there, he wrote three books. His first, *Go Tell It on the Mountain,* is a novel about a sensitive teenager in Harlem, and is considered one of his best works. After returning to the United States in 1957, he divided his time between a home in southern France and one in New York City. He died in France in 1987.

The selection you are about to read, "My Dungeon Shook," is taken from a collection of essays entitled *The Fire Next Time.* This letter to his nephew reflects James Baldwin's deep commitment to the Civil Rights Movement of the 1960s.

My Dungeon Shook

by James Baldwin

Dear James:

I have begun this letter five times and torn it up five times. I keep seeing your face, which is also the face of your father and my brother. Like him, you are tough, dark, vulnerable, moody—with a very definite tendency to sound truculent[1] because you want no one to think you are soft. You may be like your grandfather in this, I don't know, but certainly both you and your father resemble him very much physically. Well, he is dead, he never saw you, and he had a terrible life; he was defeated long before he died because, at the bottom of his heart, he really believed what white people said about him. This is one of the reasons he became so holy. I am sure that your father has told you something about all that. Neither you nor your father exhibit any tendency towards holiness: you really *are* of another era, part of what happened when the Negro left the land and came into what the late E. Franklin Frazier[2] called "the cities of destruction." You can only be destroyed by believing that you really are what the white

---

1. **truculent** (TRUK-yoo-luhnt) *adj.* ferocious; fierce
2. **E. Franklin Frazier** (FRAY-zher) a historian, sociologist, and university professor, considered an authority on the African American family, who lived from 1894 to 1962

world calls a *nigger*. I tell you this because I love you, and please don't you ever forget it.

I have known both of you all your lives, have carried your Daddy in my arms and on my shoulders, kissed and spanked him and watched him learn to walk. I don't know if you've known anybody from that far back; if you've loved anybody that long, first as an infant, then as a child, then as a man, you gain a strange perspective on time and human pain and effort. Other people cannot see what I see whenever I look into your father's face, for behind your father's face as it is today are all those other faces which were his. Let him laugh and I see a cellar your father does not remember and a house he does not remember and I hear in his present laughter his laughter as a child. Let him curse and I remember him falling down the cellar steps, and howling, and I remember, with pain, his tears, which my hand or your grandmother's so easily wiped away. But no one's hand can wipe away those tears he sheds invisibly today, which one hears in his laughter and in his speech and in his songs. I know what the world has done to my brother and how narrowly he has survived it. And I know, which is much worse, and this is the crime of which I accuse my country and my countrymen, and for which neither I nor time nor history will ever forgive them, that they have destroyed and are destroying hundreds of thousands of lives and do not know it and do not want to know it. One can be, indeed one must strive to become, tough and philosophical concerning destruction and death, for this is what most of mankind has been best at since we have heard of man. (But remember: *most* of mankind is not *all* of mankind.) But it is not permissible that the authors of devastation should also be innocent. It is the innocence which constitutes the crime.

Now, my dear namesake, these innocent and well-meaning people, your countrymen, have caused you to be born under conditions not very far removed from those described for us by Charles Dickens[3] in the London of more than a hundred years ago. (I hear the chorus of the innocents screaming, "No! This is not true! How *bitter* you are!"—but I am writing this letter to *you*, to try to tell you something about how to handle *them,* for most of them do not yet really know that you exist. I *know* the conditions under which you were born, for I was there. Your countrymen were *not* there, and haven't made it yet. Your grandmother was also there, and no one has ever accused her of being bitter. I suggest that the innocents check with her. She isn't hard to find. Your countrymen don't know that *she* exists, either, though she has been working for them all their lives.)

Well, you were born, here you came, something like fourteen years ago; and though your father and mother and grandmother, looking about the streets through which they were carrying you, staring at the walls into which they brought you, had every reason to be heavyhearted, yet they were not. For here you were, Big James, named for me— you were a big baby, I was not—here you were: to be loved. To be loved, baby, hard, at once, and forever, to strengthen you against the loveless world. Remember that: I know how black it looks today, for you. It looked bad that day, too, yes, we were trembling. We have not stopped trembling yet, but if we had not loved each other none of us would have survived. And now you must survive because we love you, and for the sake of your children and your children's children.

This innocent country set you down in a ghetto[4] in

---

3. **Charles Dickens** (DIHK-ihnz) a popular English novelist who lived from 1812 to 1870 and whose books often portrayed the miserable living conditions of Londoners
4. **ghetto** (GEHT-oh) *n.* a section of a city occupied by members of the same ethnic group

which, in fact, it intended that you should perish. Let me spell out precisely what I mean by that, for the heart of the matter is here, and the root of my dispute with my country. You were born where you were born and faced the future that you faced because you were black and *for no other reason*. The limits of your ambition were, thus, expected to be set forever. You were born into a society which spelled out with brutal clarity, and in as many ways as possible, that you were a worthless human being. You were not expected to aspire to excellence: you were expected to make peace with mediocrity. Wherever you have turned, James, in your short time on this earth, you have been told where you could go and what you could do (and *how* you could do it) and where you could live and whom you could marry. I know your countrymen do not agree with me about this, and I hear them saying, "You exaggerate." They do not know Harlem, and I do. So do you. Take no one's word for anything, including mine—but trust your experience. Know whence you came. If you know whence you came, there is really no limit to where you can go. The details and symbols of your life have been deliberately constructed to make you believe what white people say about you. Please try to remember that what they believe, as well as what they do and cause you to endure, does not testify to your inferiority but to their inhumanity and fear. Please try to be clear, dear James, through the storm which rages about your youthful head today, about the reality which lies behind the words *acceptance and integration*. There is no reason for you to try to become like white people and there is no basis whatever for their impertinent assumption that *they* must accept *you*. The really terrible thing, old buddy, is that *you* must accept *them*. And I mean that very seriously. You must accept them and accept them with love. For these innocent people have no other hope. They are, in effect, still trapped in a history which they do

not understand; and until they understand it, they cannot
be released from it. They have had to believe for many
years, and for innumerable reasons, that black men are
inferior to white men. Many of them, indeed, know better,
but, as you will discover, people find it very difficult to act
on what they know. To act is to be committed, and to be
committed is to be in danger. In this case, the danger, in
the minds of most white Americans, is the loss of their
identity. Try to imagine how you would feel if you woke up
one morning to find the sun shining and all the stars
aflame. You would be frightened because it is out of the
order of nature. Any upheaval in the universe is terrifying
because it so profoundly attacks one's sense of one's own
reality. Well, the black man has functioned in the white
man's world as a fixed star, as an immovable pillar: and as
he moves out of his place, heaven and earth are shaken to
their foundations. You, don't be afraid. I said that it was
intended that you should perish in the ghetto, perish by
never being allowed to go behind the white man's
definitions, by never being allowed to spell your proper
name. You have, and many of us have, defeated this
intention; and, by a terrible law, a terrible paradox,[5] those
innocents who believed that your imprisonment made
them safe are losing their grasp of reality. But these men
are your brothers—your lost, younger brothers. And if the
word *integration* means anything, this is what it means: that
we, with love, shall force our brothers to see themselves as
they are, to cease fleeing from reality and begin to change
it. For this is your home, my friend, do not be driven from
it; great men have done great things here, and will again,
and we can make America what America must become. It
will be hard, James, but you come from sturdy, peasant

---

5. **paradox** (PAR-uh-dahks) *n.* a statement that seems contradictory

stock, men who picked cotton and dammed rivers and built railroads, and, in the teeth of the most terrifying odds, achieved an unassailable and monumental dignity. You come from a long line of great poets, some of the greatest poets since Homer.[6] One of them said, *The very time I thought I was lost, My dungeon shook and my chains fell off.*

You know, and I know, that the country is celebrating one hundred years of freedom one hundred years too soon.[7] We cannot be free until they are free. God bless you, James, and Godspeed.

Your uncle,
James

---

6. **Homer** (HOH-muhr) an ancient Greek poet who wrote the great epic poems *The Iliad* and *The Odyssey*
7. A reference to Abraham Lincoln's famous Emancipation Proclamation, which, as of January 1, 1863, freed the slaves

AFTER YOU READ

Exchanging Backgrounds and Cultures

1. How has society in the United States formed a dungeon for African Americans?

2. Despite negative circumstances, what strengths does James Baldwin see in African American culture?

3. What is Baldwin's hope for his nephew's generation?

What Do You Think?

Which part of James Baldwin's letter do you think is most effective? Why? How does the letter apply to your own life?

Experiencing Nonfiction

In writing this letter, James Baldwin wants his nephew to believe in his own worth, to avoid the trap of believing what others say about him. Have you ever felt misjudged by someone? How did you respond? Write an autobiographical sketch about your experience.

Optional Activity Write a letter to a special person who has helped you to believe in yourself. Include in your letter the circumstances in which that person helped you and a description of the effect he or she had on you.

INTRODUCTION
The Long Shadow
of Little Rock

Elizabeth Eckford, born in 1942, grew up in troubled times. She was a girl of 12 in 1954 when the U.S. Supreme Court handed down its famous decision in the landmark case, *Brown* v. *Board of Education*. It was this case that banned segregation in public schools. The next year, Rosa Parks refused to give her bus seat to a white passenger, thus igniting the Civil Rights Movement.

Then, in September 1957, Elizabeth and eight other African American students made history. They were to enter Central High School in Little Rock, Arkansas, as part of a court-ordered integration plan. Because of the buildup of tension and anger, plans were suddenly changed, but Elizabeth was not notified. In the meantime, the governor had ordered Arkansas National Guardsmen to surround the school and prevent the African American students from entering. This was done to preserve order, the governor claimed. On the morning of September 4, Elizabeth was on her own, and was terrified. This is her account of that day.

from *The Long Shadow of Little Rock*

as told to Daisy Bates by Elizabeth Eckford

"The day before we were to go in, we met Superintendent Blossom at the school board office. He told us what the mob might say and do but he never told us we wouldn't have any protection. He told our parents not to come because he wouldn't be able to protect the children if they did.

"That night I was so excited I couldn't sleep. The next morning I was about the first one up. While I was pressing my black and white dress—I had made it to wear on the first day of school—my little brother turned on the TV set. They started telling about a large crowd gathered at the school. The man on TV said he wondered if we were going to show up that morning. Mother called from the kitchen, where she was fixing breakfast. 'Turn that TV off!' She was so upset and worried. I wanted to comfort her, so I said, 'Mother, don't worry.'

"Dad was walking back and forth, from room to room, with a sad expression. He was chewing on his pipe and he had a cigar in his hand, but he didn't light either one. It would have been funny, only he was nervous.

"Before I left home Mother called us into the livingroom. She said we should have a word of prayer. Then I caught the bus and got off a block from the school.

I saw a large crowd of people standing across the street from the soldiers guarding Central. As I walked on, the crowd suddenly got very quiet. Superintendent Blossom had told us to enter by the front door. I looked at all the people and thought, 'Maybe I will be safer if I walk down the block to the front entrance behind the guards.'

"At the corner I tried to pass through the long line of guards around the school so as to enter the grounds behind them. One of the guards pointed across the street. So I pointed in the same direction and asked whether he meant for me to cross the street and walk down. He nodded 'yes.' So I walked across the street conscious of the crowd that stood there, but they moved away from me.

"For a moment all I could hear was the shuffling of their feet. Then someone shouted, 'Here she comes, get ready!' I moved away from the crowd on the sidewalk and into the street. If the mob came at me I could then cross back over so the guards could protect me.

"The crowd moved in closer and then began to follow me, calling me names. I still wasn't afraid. Just a little bit nervous. Then my knees started to shake all of a sudden and I wondered whether I could make it to the center entrance a block away. It was the longest block I ever walked in my whole life.

"Even so, I still wasn't too scared because all the time I kept thinking that the guards would protect me.

"When I got right in front of the school, I went up to a guard again. But this time he just looked straight ahead and didn't move to let me pass him. I didn't know what to do. Then I looked and saw that the path leading to the front entrance was a little further ahead. So I walked until I was right in front of the path to the front door.

"I stood looking at the school—it looked so big! Just then the guards let some white students go through.

"The crowd was quiet. I guess they were waiting to see

what was going to happen. When I was able to steady my knees, I walked up to the guard who had let the white students in. He too didn't move. When I tried to squeeze past him, he raised his bayonet[1] and then the other guards closed in and they raised their bayonets.

"They glared at me with a mean look and I was very frightened and didn't know what to do. I turned around and the crowd came toward me.

"They moved closer and closer. Somebody started yelling, 'Lynch her! Lynch her!'

"I tried to see a friendly face somewhere in the mob—someone who maybe would help. I looked into the face of an old woman and it seemed a kind face, but when I looked at her again, she spat on me.

"They came closer, shouting, 'No nigger . . . is going to get in our school. Get out of here!'

"I turned back to the guards, but their faces told me I wouldn't get help from them. Then I looked down the block and saw a bench at the bus stop. I thought, 'If I can only get there I will be safe.' I don't know why the bench seemed like a safe place to me, but I started walking toward it. I tried to close my mind to what they were shouting, and kept saying to myself, 'If I can only make it to that bench I will be safe.'

"When I finally got there, I don't think I could have gone another step. I sat down and the mob crowded up and began shouting all over again. Someone hollered, 'Drag her over to this tree! Let's take care of this nigger.' Just then a white man sat down beside me, put his arm around me and patted my shoulder. He raised my chin and said, 'Don't let them see you cry.'

---

1. **bayonet** (bay-uh-NEHT) *n.* a detachable, daggerlike blade on the end of a rifle

"Then a white lady—she was very nice—she came over to me on the bench. She spoke to me but I don't remember now what she said. She put me on the bus and sat next to me. She asked me my name and tried to talk to me but I don't think I answered. I can't remember much about the bus ride, but the next thing I remember I was standing in front of the School for the Blind, where Mother works.

"I thought, 'Maybe she isn't here. But she has to be here!' So I ran upstairs, and I think some teachers tried to talk to me, but I kept running until I reached Mother's classroom.

"Mother was standing at the window with her head bowed, but she must have sensed I was there because she turned around. She looked as if she had been crying, and I wanted to tell her I was all right. But I couldn't speak. She put her arms around me and I cried."

AFTER YOU READ

Exchanging Backgrounds and Cultures

1. How were Elizabeth's feelings different from her parents' feelings on the morning of September 4? Why do you think their feelings were so different?

2. How would you characterize society in Little Rock in 1957?

3. Even though this is a short excerpt, what does it show about Elizabeth's family?

What Do You Think?

Do you think it was more difficult for a young person like Elizabeth to undergo this experience than it would have been for an adult? Why?

Experiencing Nonfiction

Have you or someone you know made it through a difficult experience like Elizabeth's with the help of friends or family? Write a brief account of that experience, making sure that you provide any background that is necessary for understanding the situation.

Optional Activity Write a brief biographical account about a well-known historical figure whom you admire who showed courage when faced with a difficult situation. Focus on one incident, and be sure the details you include are accurate.

INTRODUCTION
Waiting for Malcolm

Ja Jahannes was born in Fredericksburg, Virginia, in 1942, the son of the county's first African American policeman. Jahannes has traced the origin of his name to Ethiopia and Nigeria. Jahannes was educated at Lincoln University in Pennsylvania, Hampton University in Virginia, and the University of Delaware. He has traveled and taught in Africa, Asia, and Latin America. Jahannes has received many awards and honors, including the Langston Hughes Cultural Arts Award.

Jahannes has many talents. He is a scholar, psychologist, ordained minister, poet, and playwright. All these vocations, he says, are about healing. "He speaks to problems in the black community that don't always get a lot of time," reports Professor Hanes Walton of Savannah State College.

In the following essay, Jahannes tells about hearing Malcolm X speak. Jahannes was fascinated by the man and his message. Using the power of poetic language, Jahannes tells how this one encounter changed his life.

from Waiting for Malcolm

by Ja A. Jahannes

◆
◆
◆ I was waiting for Malcolm X on a January evening in the Mary Dodd Memorial Chapel[1] in 1963. Cold, white snow covered the rolling hills of southern Chester County but an air of warm expectancy filled the sanctuary.

I was a twenty year old black man-child.

I waited for Malcolm to bring together those ideas I had been taught in the schools of America and on the streets.

I was not falling. I was not sinking. I was not reeling. It was not like anything I could describe. It was like none of those sensations I remembered in the bad dreams of my youth. It was like breathing water. Like standing still as the world jerked to a halt. All sound was snuffed out. All fear anesthetized.[2] Suddenly I could hear the train. Not hear as I was used to hearing. A knowing. A beyond sense reckoning of the presence of the train. The inevitable, inescapable pull of the train transcended universes of truth. Like a monster of possession let loose to rendezvous[3] with this moment, the train was coming.

---

1. **Mary Dodd Memorial Chapel** located at Lincoln University in Oxford, Pennsylvania
2. **anesthetized** (uh-NEHS-thuh-teyezd) *v.* caused a loss of the sense of pain
3. **rendezvous** (RAHN-day-voo) *v.* to meet at a certain time or place

Malcolm was speaking. My life retreated to a punctuation mark. I was perfectly conscious. . . .

Malcolm was speaking.

The train was steady on its destination. Time and circumstance were being reduced to an equation outside of science. Doubt ran like a mad dog howling at the chaos in the universe.

It hit me. The unalterable truth hit me. I had known it all my life. It was written in the roots of my existence on the planet. It was a fundamental truth older than written history. It was super-ordinary to all the rituals that had been devised to keep the people in check through all the millennia.[4] It was an unalterable truth. Black folks would not commit their own genocide.[5]

Malcolm was speaking. His voice was actually pleasant. It was inviting. It did not threaten. The train was coming.

Who could predict that Malcolm would become the pop image icon[6] of the future generations of conscious Blacks, would be looking out at the world from an oversized face on the front of the new fashion, eyes blazing.

Malcolm's eyes seared. They were full of the hurt that generations of Blacks had felt in America. Deprivation. Defeat. Malcolm's face would be on more t-shirts than Martin King, Michael Jordan, Magic Johnson, Michael Jackson, Spike Lee and Prince.[7]

---

4. **millennia** (mih-LEHN-nee-uh) *n. pl.* thousands of years
5. **genocide** (JEHN-uh-seyed) *n.* the purposeful killing of a whole national or ethnic group of people
6. **icon** (EYE-kahn) *n.* someone who is the object of great attention; an idol
7. **Martin (Luther) King (Jr.)** famous civil rights leader; **Michael Jordan** and **Magic Johnson** professional basketball players; **Michael Jackson** popular singer; **Spike Lee** film director; **Prince** popular singer; all African Americans

Malcolm would peer out on an ugly, unaccepting, and uncaring world. A world that had rejected him because he was too prone to speak the truth even under penalty of death. Malcolm's eyes would also reflect a deep love. The very power of the man was love. The extraordinary love for self. That self love that is fundamental to the ability to love your brothers and sisters, to love your neighbors as yourself.

Suddenly nothing happened. Time stopped. It was absurdly quiet.

Then I heard the train. It was coming through Mary Dodd Memorial Chapel. It was coming through the walls. It was coming down on me. It was coming through my brain.

Malcolm stood at the podium fully in command of himself and his audience.

This train is bound for Glory, this train.[8]

The next evening my English professor asked me what I thought of Malcolm. Did I think it was wise to bring such a hatemonger to the university?

"I agreed with everything he said," I responded. "He was right on the money." While I sat there dining at this *white* professor's table, I confessed that Malcolm had inspired me as no other man in my life. Why? Because Malcolm was so bold with the truth.

Malcolm had done his homework before he came to speak at the university. He had cased the joint. Or somebody had got the scoop for him. It didn't matter. The point was he knew what was going on. A message ain't worth spit if it is out there somewhere other than where the audience lives. Malcolm wasn't like that.

From the moment Malcolm started speaking I was on fire. I was bewitched. Those eyes. That voice. The train.

---

8. lyrics from "This Train," a spiritual, or religious folk song of African American origin

Malcolm mesmerized me with his sureness—borne of living on the edge of alienation. He enthralled me with his prophecy. Prophets are supposed to be without honor in their own country. I honored Malcolm in the country of my soul.

I felt Malcolm's prophecy. It was a sacred drum beating in my soul. America was messed up because white folks messed over Black folks. America could only begin to become healthy when Black folks rescued their psyches.[9] Then Black folks would learn to negotiate their economic freedom. It was as simple as that. A whole lot of people knew the truth, but they were afraid to admit it to themselves or let it pass their lips.

There was Malcolm boldly proclaiming the truth. He was some *bad*[10] brother. And he had started by mocking the civil rights work I had busted my butt doing in the harsh winter cold.

Mind you, I did not think Malcolm was some quintessential orator. I had heard great orators regularly—especially at Lincoln University—that would put Malcolm to shame. I had heard Rabbi Martin Weitz,[11] whose orations were Coltrane[12] rhapsodies, painted in word tapestries that were pure art. I had heard clergymen, political types, and actors lift the rafters in oratorical elegance. And weekly I was privileged to hear university professors soar in the old school oratory that owed its wings to the best traditions of the Negro preacher and the Princeton-Yale forensic[13] style. I had heard real oratory.

---

9. **psyches** (SEYE-keez) *n. pl.* spirits or souls
10. *bad* (BAD) *adj.* (slang) great
11. **Rabbi Martin Weitz** (WEYETS) a Jewish religious leader, educator, and author who was born in 1907
12. **Coltrane** (KOHL-trayn) John Coltrane, a famous jazz saxophonist and composer who lived from 1926 to 1967
13. **forensic** (fuh-REHN-sihk) *adj.* debating

Malcolm was only an above average speaker by comparison. But he had one power over the others. Truth. His truth was like a sword. It unsheathed itself and cut into the heart.

Malcolm knocked the feet out from under me. He stood there and questioned the protest movement which I had been leading to desegregate the movie theaters and public facilities in Wilmington, Delaware. Made more sense, he said, to educate the Black citizens of Wilmington and the other surrounding cities on U.S. Route 40 on how they could pull themselves out of the poverty that engulfed them. Said those poor Black folks could barely afford to go to those movies even if they were admitted. I grasped the truth of what he was saying. Teach Malcolm. Teach Malcolm. I kept hearing the train. Teach Malcolm.

"You would be one of the first ones I would have to deny," I heard myself saying in even tones to my English professor. His wife looked on in amazement. Intuitively, I knew she was thinking, "You see, you cannot do too much for these Negroes; they will never appreciate it, they will betray you." I never felt that she was committed to her husband's relationship with me or the other Black students at the university. Especially with me. It was a kind of gut feeling. Sometimes you just know in your gut that the vibe isn't right.

"And why would that be?" the professor had asked, showing his irritation despite himself. I could see that the professor was controlling his anger. What had made me so bold? What had made me say things that would hurt this man who was truly my friend, my teacher, my mentor? It was Malcolm's truth. Truth boarded itself.

I was feeling uneasy too. I was feeling uncomfortable. Truth often makes us feel that way. That is why we avoid it. But truth does not go away. The more you stray from truth the greater the danger of losing your mind. This is what Malcolm had given me on that cold January evening in 1963. He had given me the vision to see truth from which I could never again hide. Nothing can destroy Malcolm's truth.

"Because you are the most dangerous to me," I said calmly. "If the revolution comes, which Malcolm X is calling for, it would be wise if we denied all our good white friends first so that we would not lose our resolve."

He looked at me like I was crazy. I did not remember the rest of the evening. It became blurred. Somewhere before the evening was over I tried to explain the logic of Malcolm's speech in the pure intellectual terms of world history, how other people had thrown off their oppressors. Intellectualism was out of the window now to my teacher. And the wife never forgave me.

It was a quiet, uneasy ride in the professor's car back to the dormitory. I had often been invited to dinner at the professor's house, more often on Sunday afternoon. I wondered now was the invitation this weekday evening following Malcolm's speech on the campus a deliberate invitation to help the professor get a handle on Malcolm. It certainly was a turning point for me. I realized how afraid some white folks are of the truth.

I loved the professor. He was a good man. His heart was in the right place. The professor really did enjoy empowering my mind. Unfortunately, he was limited by the circumstances of his own life. My freedom was limited by his ignorance of the conditions of Black people in America. The professor could not understand that this ignorance was dangerous to my existence. What I really needed from him was his example. He should have been attacking his own kind who treated Black people unjustly. He could have stood with Malcolm. He could have stood with the truth.

I would never escape from the truth of race in America. Malcolm taught me that if a man does not know what killed his father he will die of the same thing.

Funny no one approves of my assertive behavior as a Black man. Funny no one gives me rave reviews for not acting like a wimp. Whenever I speak up, I am too outspoken. Whenever I am forceful, I am too strident.[14] Whenever I am passionate, I am too emotional. Whenever I am assertive, I am too aggressive. But Malcolm taught me to stand like a man.

I had been waiting for the train. Truth was on the rails.

This train is bound for Glory, this train.

---

14. **strident** (STREYED-uhnt) *adj.* harsh; noisy

AFTER YOU READ

Exchanging Backgrounds and Cultures

1. What metaphor does Jahannes use repeatedly to describe the effect of Malcolm X's words on him? Why do you think he chose it?

2. What personal conflicts did Malcolm's words create for Jahannes?

3. How does this account reflect the author's pride as an African American?

What Do You Think?

What effect did this autobiographical essay have on you? What effect do you think the author intended?

Experiencing Nonfiction

In his autobiographical essay, Jahannes tells how someone else's words affected him. Think about an incident in which someone's words had an important effect on you—the words of a poet, an author, a songwriter, a speaker, or someone you know. In a brief essay, tell about reading or hearing those words and explain how they affected you.

Optional Activity Ja Jahannes used poetic language to show how intense his feelings were as he listened to Malcolm X. Think of an experience that affected you deeply. Write a brief essay that captures your feelings about the incident, using one or more central images.

INTRODUCTION
Sweet Summer

Born in 1950, Bebe Moore Campbell grew up in two places, in two different worlds, North and South. During the winter she lived in Philadelphia, Pennsylvania, with her mother and grandmother and attended an integrated school, Logan Elementary. But summers she spent in North Carolina with her father, surrounded by her southern relatives. From her college-educated mother, Moore learned to be the best she could be. From her dad, who had been paralyzed in a car accident, she learned about determination and dignity.

Bebe Campbell is a journalist and lives in Los Angeles. In the following excerpt from her book, she tells about an incident in school that heightened her self-awareness as a young African American.

from *Sweet Summer*

by Bebe Moore Campbell

The blare of Monday's late bell jolted the last vestiges of torpor[1] from my bones. In September I had entered 5A. In January 1961 I skipped 5B and went to the sixth grade. Most of my fifth-grade classmates accompanied me to Miss Tracy's room. The Philadelphia school system, in order to end midyear graduations, had abandoned the A/B grade levels. In January most students were skipped into the next grade, although some were retained.

Miss Tracy nodded her head and held out her hands, letting her palms face her students; she drew her hands upward. I rose with the rest of the class and placed my hand over my heart, shifting my weight from foot to foot and staring straight ahead at the bulletin boards, which were still covered with red and green construction-paper Santa Clauses and Christmas trees. I acted as if I were speaking, but when the rest of the class said, "I pledge allegiance to the flag . . ." I only mouthed the words. Months before, Reverend Lewis had told the congregation that Negroes in the South were being beaten by white people because they wanted to integrate lunch counters at drugstores. A few weeks earlier, while Mommy, Nana, Michael and I were sitting in the living room watching

---

1. **torpor** (TAWR-puhr) *n.* sluggishness

television, the show was interrupted; the announcer showed colored people trying to march and white policemen coming after them with giant German shepherds.

"Now you know that ain't right," Nana had said angrily.

The day after I saw that news bulletin I was saying the Pledge of Allegiance in class and right in the middle of it my head started hurting so bad I thought it was gonna fall off and I felt so mad I wanted to punch somebody. I didn't want to say the pledge, that was the problem. I was afraid not to say anything, so I just kept opening my mouth, but nothing came out. After that I only pretended to say the words. If they were gonna sic[2] dogs on Negroes then I wasn't gonna say some pledge and I wasn't gonna sing "The Star-Spangled Banner" neither. Not for them, I wasn't.

Sixth grade was rough. In the first place, I didn't like Miss Tracy. None of my friends liked her either. She was the meanest teacher I ever had, so full of rules and ultimatums.[3] No talking. No erasures on spelling tests. No going to the bathroom except at recess. No this, no that. Always use her name when addressing her. No, Miss Frankenstein. Yes, Miss Frankenstein. She sent Linda out of the room just because she said "Excuse me" to me when she dropped my spelling paper. I mean . . . really. I could see Linda through the small glass window in the door, standing outside in the hall crying while we graded the spelling papers. Causing my best friend's tears was enough for me to start hating Miss Tracy, but I had other reasons.

It was a year of hot breathing and showdowns at Logan. We were sixth-graders, on our way out the door and feeling our oats every step of the way. . . . We were embarrassed; we were proud. But the little band of Negroes at Logan felt something more than puberty.

---

2. **sic** (SIHK) *v.* to urge to attack
3. **ultimatums** (ul-tuh-MAY-tuhmz) *n.pl.* final statements of demand that threaten serious penalties if not met

Fierce new rhythms—bam de bam de *bam bam bam!*—were welling up inside us. We were figuring things out. At home in the living room with our parents we watched the nightly news—the dogs, the hoses and nightsticks against black flesh—and we seethed; we brought our anger to school. The rumor flew around North Philly, West Philly and Germantown that Elvis Presley[4] had said, "All colored people can do for me is buy my records and shine my shoes." In the schoolyard and the classroom we saw the sea of white surrounding us and we drew in closer. We'd been fooling ourselves. It didn't matter how capable we were: it was *their* school, *their* neighborhood, *their* country, *their* planet. We were the outsiders and they looked down on us. Our bitterness exploded like an overdue time bomb.

"Miss Tracy doesn't like Negroes," I announced to Carol and Linda when we sat under the poplar tree at recess.

Linda got excited. "How do you know that?"

"You ever notice how she never picks us to do anything? And she's always putting our names on the board for talking and she doesn't ever put David's name on the board and all he does is run his mouth . . ."

"And try to act like his Elvis Presley," Carol added. "Miss Tracy's always calling us 'you people.' And remember that time she sent Wallace to the office when that white boy stepped on his foot?"

"That doesn't mean she doesn't like Negroes," Linda said doubtfully. Carol and I looked at each other and shook our heads. What a baby.

"Well, what does it mean, then?" I asked Linda sarcastically.

"It means she doesn't like the Negroes in her room," Carol said dryly.

---

4. Elvis Presley (EHL-vihs PREHS-lee) (1935–1977) an American rock- and-roll singer who greatly influenced popular culture

The skirmishes were slight affairs, nothing anyone could really put a finger on. A black boy pushed a white boy in line. A black girl muttered "cracker" when a white girl touched her accidentally. One afternoon when David was walking past our tree Carol yelled, "Elvis Presley ain't doing nothing but imitating colored people. And he can't even sing." David looked at her in astonishment. She put her hands on her hips and declared, "I ain't buying his records and I ain't shining his shoes neither!"

"Boys and girls, you're growing up," Miss Tracy said to the class one afternoon. Yes, we were. Something hot and electric was in the air.

The winter before I graduated from Logan Elementary, there was a disturbance in my class. Miss Tracy was absent and we had a substitute, a small, pretty woman named Mrs. Brown. She had taught us before, and all of us liked her because if we finished our work she would let us play hangman. We were spelling that day, going through our list of words in the usual, boring way. Mrs. Brown picked someone and the person had to go to the blackboard and write a sentence using the spelling word. We had three more words to go and I'd already been picked, so my interest in the whole process was waning. Hurry up, I thought. I was only half listening when I heard Mrs. Brown ask Clarence, who was wearing his everyday uniform, a suit and a tie, to stop talking. Clarence turned a little in his chair and frowned. He continued to talk.

"Did you hear me, Clarence?" Mrs. Brown asked.

"No."

Everybody turned to stare at Clarence and to check him for any outward signs of mental instability. Nobody talked back to teachers at Logan. Mrs. Brown coughed for a full minute, then stood up and asked Clarence to go to the board. Her voice was sharp. Clarence slouched in his seat. "No," he said almost lazily. Nobody breathed. Mrs. Brown said he would have to go to the principal's office if he wouldn't behave. All of us in class shuddered as if we were one body. Was Clarence crazy? I thought of my own dark trek to the principal's office. Nobody wanted to visit Jennie G. Clarence glared at Mrs. Brown so forcefully that she turned away from him. Clarence said slowly, "Later for the principal. Later for you. Later for all y'all white people. Send me to the principal. That don't cut no cheese with me."

Everything happened fast after that, after it was clear that Clarence had lost his mind. Mrs. Brown quickly dispatched one of the boys to bring Mr. Singer, who appeared moments later at the door. Mrs. Brown conferred with Mr. Singer hastily and then he took Clarence by the arm and ushered him out of the room. Clarence did a diddy-bop hoodlum[5] stroll and showed not one bit of remorse as he left.

As soon as he was gone, Mrs. Brown leaned back in her chair and put the sides of her hands to her temples. The small diamond on her finger glittered in the sunlight. "Why would he say such awful things to me? Why?" she demanded, looking at the class. "Why?" she repeated, her eyes now focusing on every dark face in the class as if we alone knew the answer. Everyone was looking at Linda, Carol, Wallace, and me, I realized. And they were . . . scared. Their eyes asked: Are you like Clarence? Are you angry too? Mrs. Brown tried to start the lesson again, but nobody was concentrating. Linda, Carol and I looked at each other cautiously. It was silently agreed: we wouldn't explain anything.

"That nigger's crazy!" Wallace whispered as we filed outside for recess. There was no more that could be said.

In the schoolyard, in our compact circle, we whooped like renegades. "He sure told Mrs. Brown off!" we exclaimed, falling all over each other in our excitement. "Later for all y'all white people," we repeated that single line, giggling as we slapped each other's thighs. I thought not of the dogs and the nightsticks, but of the ponytails

---

5. **hoodlum** (HŎŎD-luhm) *n.* a tough, often aggressive youngster

and poodle skirts on *Bandstand*,[6] bobbing and swishing off beat, twisting and turning so happily. Carol, Linda and I nodded at each other. The single vein of anger that was growing in us all had been acknowledged this day. We had a crazy nigger in our midst, close enough for comfort.

Clarence, of course, was suspended. A much more subdued boy returned to school flanked by his mother and father. The grapevine said that Jennie G. had said sternly to his parents, "We will not tolerate that kind of rude, uncivilized behavior at Logan. Is that clear?" When it was all over, Clarence had to apologize to Mrs. Brown and tell her he didn't know what on earth had gotten into him. But I knew.

I turned eleven in February. My father drove to Philadelphia to celebrate, and he took my mother and me to dinner at Horn & Hardart[7] because the aisles were wide enough for his wheelchair. After we ate I got behind Daddy and pushed him, and we all went around the corner to the movies. The usher stared when Daddy came in, and said, "Now you aren't gonna block up the aisle, are you?"

Mommy looked straight ahead past the man. Daddy stuck out his chin a little, laughed and said, "Where would you like me to sit, mister?" I could tell he was mad. We ended up sitting in the back. Daddy hopped into the aisle chair and folded up his chair and leaned it against the outside of his seat. I sat next to him and every time something funny or exciting happened, I squeezed Daddy's hand until I was sure he wasn't angry anymore.

We came straight home after the movie. After my father parked the car in front of our house, my parents

---

6. ***Bandstand*** a reference to the television show "American Bandstand," hosted by Dick Clark and especially popular in the 1950s and early 1960s
7. **Horn & Hardart** (HAWRN & HAHR-dahrt) a popular, inexpensive restaurant chain where customers took food from small compartments that opened after coins were put into slots

handed me a small box. Inside was a thin Timex watch with a black strap. I gasped with happiness and excitement. I was sitting between my mother and father, admiring my watch, basking in their adoration. I'd forgotten all about the usher. This is the way it should always be, I thought. When my mother said it was time for us to go in I said, "Kiss Daddy."

Mommy paused for a moment. My father looked awkward. He leaned toward my mother. She pecked him on the cheek.

"No. Not like that," I chided them. "Kiss on the lips."

They obeyed me and gave each other another brief, chaste peck. Why couldn't they kiss better than that? Mr. Johnston wasn't my mother's boyfriend anymore. He hadn't been around for several months. Why couldn't she love my daddy again? My mother and father didn't look at each other as they moved away.

I wanted magic from them, a kiss that would ignite their love, reunite all three of us. As my father drove off I looked down at my watch and stared at the minute hand ticking away.

Miss Tracy worked our butts off until just before graduation. She assigned us a health report and an arithmetic project, and we had to write a creative story using all the spelling words we'd had since January. On top of everything else, she gave us a book report.

Miss Tracy took our class to the school library and told us to find the book we wanted to do a report on and to make sure we told her what it was. I turned the library inside out trying to find a book I liked. The problem was, I'd read all the good stuff. So I asked Miss Tracy if I could get my book from the public library; she said that was fine with her.

Michael, Mommy and I went to the downtown library one Sunday after church. I searched in the young adult section for an interesting title. Then I went to where the new books were displayed and picked up one with a picture of an earnest-looking black boy in the foreground and a small town in the background. I started leafing through some of the pages and I couldn't put it down. The book was about Negroes trying to win their rights in a small southern town and how they struggled against bad white people and were helped by good ones. There weren't any bad Negroes and that fit my mood perfectly. As I was reading it, the thought hit me instantly: Miss Tracy wouldn't want me to do my report on *South Town*.[8] She'd tell me it wasn't "suitable." I decided I wouldn't tell Miss Tracy; I'd just do the report.

The day I stood in front of the class to give my report, my mouth was dry and my hands were moist. "My book is called *South Town*," I said, holding the book up so everybody could see the cover. The whole class got quiet as they studied the black boy's serious face; Miss Tracy's head jerked up straight. "This was a very exciting, dramatic book, and I liked it a lot, because every summer I live in a place exactly like the town that was described in this book," I said, my voice rising. I had my entire book report memorized and after a while everything came easily. I walked across the room, raising my hand for dramatic flair, feeling like a bold renegade telling my people's struggle to the world. I whispered when I described a sad part of the book. I finished with a flourish. "I recommend this book for anyone interested in the struggle for Negroes to gain equal rights in America. Thank you."

As soon as I sat down I could feel Miss Tracy's breath on my neck. You didn't ask my permission to do that report," she said. Her hazel eyes were as cold as windowpanes in February. I had forgotten how terrifying Miss Tracy's rage could be. What if she gave me an F? Or sent me to the principal's office? Oh, Lordy.

"I'm sorry," I said, my voice drained of dramatic flair. I didn't feel like such a bold renegade anymore. I was scared.

---

8. *South Town* an award-winning novel, published in 1958, by social worker and author Lorenz Graham

Miss Tracy turned away without saying a word. Three days later she returned the reports. At the bottom in the right-hand corner of mine there was a small B. Emblazoned across the top in fierce red ink were the words: "Learn to follow directions."

I took the report home and gave it to my mother who, of course, asked, "What directions didn't you follow?" I told her the whole story; then I held my breath. The last thing I wanted to hear was, "Bebe, I'm disappointed in you." Mommy didn't say that; she just looked at Miss Tracy's comments again. Then she said, "Sometimes you eat the bear; sometimes the bear eats you," which sounded kinda strange coming from her, because Mommy wasn't one for a lot of down-home sayings. She put the report in the bottom drawer of her bureau, where she kept my school papers and grades. "Don't worry about it," Mommy said.

Three weeks later I sat on the stage of the school auditorium in the green chiffon dress my mother made me, underneath it a brand-new Littlest Angel bra identical to the one Linda's mother had bought her. The straps cut into my shoulders, but my mind was too crowded with thoughts for me to feel any pain. As Nana, Mommy, Michael and Pete watched, I walked across the stage to receive my certificate. Pete took pictures. I wanted my father to be there, but at least I could show him the photos.

Two weeks later I kissed Mommy, Nana and Michael good-bye and climbed into my father's newest acquisition, a blue Impala convertible. "BebebebebebebebeMoore," Daddy sang out when he saw me, then, "I guess you're getting too big for that stuff, huh?" His eyes were questioning, searching. I didn't know what to say, afraid that if I said yes, Daddy would never again make a song of my name, and if I said no, he'd think of me as a baby forever. So I leaned my head back against the seat and smiled. The wind was in my face and I was heading toward a North Carolina summer that would deliver a heartbreak and a promise.

AFTER YOU READ

Exchanging Backgrounds and Cultures

1. What contradiction did Bebe Campbell see between saying the Pledge of Allegiance in school and the events she heard about or saw on the news?

2. Why did Bebe choose *South Town* for a book report? What does her choice tell you about her feelings about herself?

3. What importance do you think the incidents in this selection had for the author?

What Do You Think?

Which part of this account was most meaningful to you? Why?

Experiencing Nonfiction

One of the challenges of growing up is getting adults to listen to you and acknowledge that your thoughts, opinions, and feelings are important. For Bebe Campbell and her African American classmates, this was doubly difficult in a racially divided society. Write a brief autobiographical account about a conflict in your life that helped you understand yourself better.

Optional Activity Bebe Campbell felt like an outsider in her school. Many young people, at some time or another and for a variety of reasons, feel as though they are on the outside looking in. Write a brief essay—autobiographical or general—that shows or discusses the effects that exclusion has on people.

UNIT 1: FOCUS ON WRITING

Nonfiction tells about real-life events, people, and places. Some types of nonfiction, such as news stories, are objective, factual accounts. Other nonfiction, however, such as Ja Jahannes's autobiographical essay, offers the author's personal interpretation of events.

Writing Nonfiction

Choose one of the following two topics: Write an autobiographical account in which you describe an important personal experience; write an essay about a topic or issue you feel strongly about.

The Writing Process

Good writing requires both time and effort. An effective writer completes a number of stages that together make up the writing process. The stages of the writing process are given below to help guide you through your assignment.

Prewriting

After you have decided what type of nonfiction you want to write, explore possible topics. There are many ways to do this. If you keep a personal journal, search through it for an experience you might like to write about. Are there any current issues of magazines in your classroom? Skim through them, looking for issues that concern you and jot them down.

Once you have chosen your topic, think about a focus for your writing. If your topic can be divided into several subtopics or incidents, select just one.

Next, consider your audience and purpose. For whom are you writing? How much background do you need to provide? Is your purpose to describe, to explain, or to persuade?

Once you have determined your audience and your purpose, generate a list of specific details or ideas relating to your topic. If, for instance, you are writing an account similar to Ja Jahannes's, list descriptive words or images that help convey your feelings about the incident.

Begin by jotting down an opening line or two, thinking about how to draw your audience in. Then sketch out your piece briefly: Jot down your details or ideas in the order in which you wish to include them. If you are writing an essay, it may help to put your ideas in outline form to clarify the relationships among ideas. Do some items seem not to fit? You may want to delete those.

Drafting and Revising

After you have organized your ideas and details, begin your first draft. Keep your audience and purpose in mind as you write. Refer to your prewriting sketch, but feel free to alter it as you write.

Writers are rarely satisfied with their first drafts. Revising, in fact, is the most important part of the writing process. One of the best ways to go about revising is to talk with another writer. Ask a friend to listen as you read aloud your work and then help you evaluate its strengths and weaknesses. You may want to make a few notes as you talk. Before you declare a piece of writing to be finished, ask yourself, "Did I accomplish my purpose? Am I happy with the beginning and ending? Does my essay feel complete?"

Proofreading and Publishing

After you have finished revising your final draft, carefully proofread your work. Correct any errors in spelling, grammar, punctuation, and capitalization. Then make a neat final copy of your work.

Consider sharing your writing with your family or classmates, or submit it to a school newspaper or literary magazine.

UNIT 2

FICTION OF THE AFRICAN AMERICANS

When writing a work of fiction, unlike nonfiction, an author generally draws characters, places, and events from his or her imagination. Although these elements may not exist in the real world, they are based on the very real experiences and knowledge of the author. Good, convincing fiction allows readers to make the connection between an imaginary work and their own experiences, beliefs, and feelings as human beings.

The short story and the novel are two forms of modern fiction. A novel is longer than a short story, but they contain the same elements. The ways in which authors use these elements, however, vary greatly. The **setting** of a story is the time and place in which it occurs. The **characters** are the people in the story. The **plot** is the events that happen as a character or characters try to solve a problem or reach a goal. The **theme** is the author's message, or what the author wants a reader to understand about the subject. The **point of view** is the outlook from which the story is told.

As you will discover, the stories in this section involve a variety of characters and settings. They are all rooted, however, in the shared culture and experiences of African Americans. As you read these stories, look for themes dealing with the importance of love in the family, pride in the African American heritage, and the struggle for equality and dignity. You will see that, despite their different plots, themes, and settings, the stories all express powerful emotions and will leave you thinking about what you have read long after you have closed this book.

Born in rural Florida, African American artist Lev T. Mills studied graphic arts and printmaking in London and Paris. In this etching, *Gemini I*, the subject gazes out at us quietly, perhaps searching for an identity. Surrounding the figure are powerful images of city life and the cultural pride that have shaped this young African American.

INTRODUCTION

The Boy Who Painted Christ Black

John Henrik Clarke has visited all but one country in Africa, and he has written or edited over 20 books on African and African American culture, politics, and history. He is a writer who is truly immersed in his own heritage.

Clarke was born in Union Springs, Alabama, in 1915 but spent his boyhood in Georgia. His arrival in New York City as a young adult in 1933 began a long, distinguished career as a writer, educator, historian, and storyteller. Dr. Clarke taught at Hunter College in New York City from 1970 to 1986. He is also a founding member of several organizations dedicated to the study of African culture and the promotion of African American arts.

The selection you are about to read is Clarke's best-known short story and has been translated into more than a dozen languages. Clearly, there is universal appeal in this story about the clash between prejudice and innocence, the dignity of a young boy, and the courage of the man he admires—his principal.

The Boy Who Painted Christ Black

by John Henrik Clarke

◇
◇ He was the smartest boy in the Muskogee County School[1]—for colored children. Everybody even remotely connected with the school knew this. The teacher always pronounced his name with profound gusto as she pointed him out as the ideal student. Once I heard her say: "If he were white he might, some day, become President." Only Aaron Crawford wasn't white; quite the contrary. His skin was so solid black that it glowed, reflecting an inner virtue that was strange, and beyond my comprehension.

In many ways he looked like something that was awkwardly put together. Both his nose and his lips seemed a trifle too large for his face. To say he was ugly would be unjust and to say he was handsome would be gross exaggeration. Truthfully, I could never make up my mind about him. Sometimes he looked like something out of a book of ancient history . . . looked as if he was left over from that magnificent era before the machine age came and marred the earth's natural beauty.

His great variety of talent often startled the teachers. This caused his classmates to look upon him with a mixed feeling of awe and envy.

---

1. **Muskogee County** (mus-KOH-jee) a county in western Georgia

Before Thanksgiving, he always drew turkeys and pumpkins on the blackboard. On George Washington's birthday, he drew large American flags surrounded by little hatchets. It was these small masterpieces that made him the most talked-about colored boy in Columbus, Georgia. The Negro principal of the Muskogee County School said he would some day be a great painter, like Henry O. Tanner.[2]

For the teacher's birthday, which fell on a day about a week before commencement, Aaron Crawford painted the picture that caused an uproar, and a turning point, at the Muskogee County School. The moment he entered the room that morning, all eyes fell on him. Besides his torn book holder, he was carrying a large-framed concern wrapped in old newspapers. As he went to his seat, the teacher's eyes followed his every motion, a curious wonderment mirrored in them conflicting with the half-smile that wreathed her face.

Aaron put his books down, then smiling broadly, advanced toward the teacher's desk. His alert eyes were so bright with joy that they were almost frightening. The children were leaning forward in their seats, staring greedily at him; a restless anticipation was rampant within every breast.

Already the teacher sensed that Aaron had a present for her. Still smiling, he placed it on her desk and began to help her unwrap it. As the last piece of paper fell from the large frame, the teacher jerked her hand away from it suddenly, her eyes flickering unbelievingly. Amidst the rigid tension, her heavy breathing was distinct and frightening. Temporarily, there was no other sound in the room.

---

2. **Henry O. Tanner** (TAN-uhr) a painter who lived from 1859 to 1937, the first African American to be given full membership in the National Academy of Art and Design

Aaron stared questioningly at her and she moved her hand back to the present cautiously, as if it were a living thing with vicious characteristics. I am sure it was the one thing she least expected.

With a quick, involuntary movement I rose up from my desk. A series of submerged murmurs spread through the room, rising to a distinct monotone. The teacher turned toward the children, staring reproachfully. They did not move their eyes from the present that Aaron had brought her. . . . It was a large picture of Christ—painted black!

Aaron Crawford went back to his seat, a feeling of triumph reflecting in his every movement.

The teacher faced us. Her curious half-smile had blurred into a mild bewilderment. She searched the bright faces before her and started to smile again, occasionally stealing quick glances at the large picture propped on her desk, as though doing so were forbidden amusement.

"Aaron," she spoke at last, a slight tinge of uncertainty in her tone, "this is a most welcome present. Thanks. I will treasure it." She paused, then went on speaking, a trifle more coherent than before. "Looks like you are going to be quite an artist . . . . Suppose you come forward and tell the class how you came to paint this remarkable picture."

When he rose to speak, to explain about the picture, a hush fell tightly over the room, and the children gave him all of their attention . . . something they rarely did for the teacher. He did not speak at first; he just stood there in front of the room, toying absently with his hands, observing his audience carefully, like a great concert artist.

"It was like this," he said, placing full emphasis on every word. "You see, my uncle who lives in New York teaches classes in Negro History at the Y.M.C.A. When he visited us last year he was telling me about the many great black folks who have made history. He said black folks were once the most powerful people on earth. When I asked him about Christ, he said no one ever proved whether he was black or white. Somehow a feeling came over me that he was a black man, 'cause he was so kind and forgiving, kinder than I have ever seen white people be. So, when I painted his picture I couldn't help but paint it as I thought it was."

After this, the little artist sat down, smiling broadly, as if he had gained entrance to a great storehouse of knowledge that ordinary people could neither acquire nor comprehend.

The teacher, knowing nothing else to do under prevailing circumstances, invited the children to rise from their seats and come forward so they could get a complete view of Aaron's unique piece of art.

When I came close to the picture, I noticed it was painted with the kind of paint you get in the five and ten cents stores. Its shape was blurred slightly, as if someone had jarred the frame before the paint had time to dry. The eyes of Christ were deepset and sad, very much like those of Aaron's father, who was a deacon in the local Baptist Church. This picture of Christ looked much different from the one I saw hanging on the wall when I was in Sunday School. It looked more like a helpless Negro, pleading silently for mercy.

For the next few days, there was much talk about Aaron's picture.

The school term ended the following week and Aaron's picture, along with the best handwork done by the students that year, was on display in the assembly room. Naturally, Aaron's picture graced the place of honor.

There was no book work to be done on commencement day and joy was rampant among the children. The girls in their brightly colored dresses gave the school the delightful air of Spring awakening.

In the middle of the day all the children were gathered in the small assembly. On this day we were always favored with a visit from a man whom all the teachers spoke of with mixed esteem and fear. Professor Danual, they called him, and they always pronounced his name with reverence. He was supervisor of all the city schools, including those small and poorly equipped ones set aside for colored children.

The great man arrived almost at the end of our commencement exercises. On seeing him enter the hall, the children rose, bowed courteously, and sat down again, their eyes examining him as if he were a circus freak.

He was a tall white man with solid gray hair that made his lean face seem paler than it actually was. His eyes were the clearest blue I have ever seen. They were the only life-like things about him.

As he made his way to the front of the room the Negro principal, George Du Vaul, was walking ahead of him, cautiously preventing anything from getting in his way. As he passed me, I heard the teachers, frightened, sucking in their breath, felt the tension tightening.

A large chair was in the center of the rostrum.[3] It had been daintily polished and the janitor had laboriously recushioned its bottom. The supervisor went straight to it without being guided, knowing that this pretty splendor was reserved for him.

Presently the Negro principal introduced the distinguished guest and he favored us with a short speech. It wasn't a very important speech. Almost at the end of it, I remembered him saying something about he wouldn't be surprised if one of us boys grew up to be a great colored man, like Booker T. Washington.[4]

---

3. **rostrum** (RAHS-truhm) *n.* a platform for public speaking
4. **Booker T. Washington** (WAWSH-ihng-tuhn) a famous African American educator who was born into slavery in 1856 and died in 1915

After he sat down, the school chorus sang two spirituals and the girls in the fourth grade did an Indian folk dance. This brought the commencement program to an end.

After this the supervisor came down from the rostrum, his eyes tinged with curiosity, and began to view the array of handwork on display in front of the chapel.

Suddenly his face underwent a strange rejuvenation.[5] His clear blue eyes flickered in astonishment. He was looking at Aaron Crawford's picture of Christ. Mechanically he moved his stooped form closer to the picture and stood gazing fixedly at it, curious and undecided, as though it were a dangerous animal that would rise any moment and spread destruction.

We waited tensely for his next movement. The silence was almost suffocating. At last he twisted himself around and began to search the grim faces before him. The fiery glitter of his eyes abated slightly as they rested on the Negro principal, protestingly.

"Who painted this sacrilegious[6] nonsense?" he demanded sharply.

"I painted it, sir." These were Aaron's words, spoken hesitantly. He wetted his lips timidly and looked up at the supervisor, his eyes voicing a sad plea for understanding.

He spoke again, this time more coherently. "Th' principal said a colored person have jes as much right paintin' Jesus black as a white person have paintin' him white. And he says. . . ." At this point he halted abruptly, as if to search for his next words. A strong tinge of bewilderment dimmed the glow of his solid black face. He stammered out a few more words, then stopped again.

The supervisor strode a few steps toward him. At

---

5. **rejuvenation** (rih-joo-vuh-NAY-shuhn) *n.* the process of seeming new or fresh again
6. **sacrilegious** (sak-ruh-LIHJ-uhs) *adj.* intentionally disrespectful toward something sacred

last color had swelled some of the lifelessness out of his lean face.

"Well, go on!" he said, enragedly, ". . . I'm still listening."

Aaron moved his lips pathetically but no words passed them. His eyes wandered around the room, resting finally, with an air of hope, on the face of the Negro principal. After a moment, he jerked his face in another direction, regretfully, as if something he had said had betrayed an understanding between him and the principal.

Presently the principal stepped forward to defend the school's prize student.

"I encouraged the boy in painting that picture," he said firmly. "And it was with my permission that he brought the picture into this school. I don't think the boy is so far wrong in painting Christ black. The artists of all other races have painted whatever God they worship to resemble themselves. I see no reason why we should be immune from that privilege. After all, Christ was born in that part of the world that had always been predominantly populated by colored people. There is a strong possibility that he could have been a Negro."

But for the monotonous lull of heavy breathing, I would have sworn that his words had frozen everyone in the hall. I had never heard the little principal speak so boldly to anyone, black or white.

The supervisor swallowed dumfoundedly. His face was aglow in silent rage.

"Have you been teaching these children things like that?" he asked the Negro principal, sternly.

"I have been teaching them that their race has produced great kings and queens as well as slaves and serfs," the principal said. "The time is long overdue when we should let the world know that we erected and enjoyed the benefits of a splendid civilization long before the people of Europe had a written language."

The supervisor coughed. His eyes bulged menacingly

as he spoke. "You are not being paid to teach such things in this school, and I am demanding your resignation for overstepping your limit as principal."

George Du Vaul did not speak. A strong quiver swept over his sullen face. He revolved himself slowly and walked out of the room towards his office. . . .

Some of the teachers followed the principal out of the chapel, leaving the crestfallen children restless and in a quandary[7] about what to do next. Finally we started back to our rooms. . . .

A few days later I heard that the principal had accepted a summer job as art instructor of a small high school somewhere in south Georgia and had gotten permission from Aaron's parents to take him along so he could continue to encourage him in his painting.

I was on my way home when I saw him leaving his office. He was carrying a large briefcase and some books tucked under his arm. He had already said good-by to all the teachers. And strangely, he did not look brokenhearted. As he headed for the large front door, he readjusted his horn-rimmed glasses, but did not look back. An air of triumph gave more dignity to his soldierly stride. He had the appearance of a man who had done a great thing, something greater than any ordinary man would do.

Aaron Crawford was waiting outside for him. They walked down the street together. He put his arms around Aaron's shoulder affectionately. He was talking sincerely to Aaron about something, and Aaron was listening, deeply earnest.

I watched them until they were so far down the street that their forms had begun to blur. Even from this distance I could see they were still walking in brisk, dignified strides, like two people who had won some sort of victory.

---

7. quandary (KWAHN-duh-ree) *n.* a state of uncertainty

AFTER YOU READ

Exchanging Backgrounds and Cultures

1. How was Aaron's perception of what he had painted different from the supervisor's? How did this reflect a double standard in society?

2. How did Aaron's uncle from New York City and his principal, George DuVaul, give him pride in his heritage?

3. What victory did Aaron and George DuVaul share?

What Do You Think?

At what point in the story did you feel most involved? What feelings did the story provoke?

Experiencing Fiction

When authors write fiction, they involve their characters in a conflict. In stories such as this one by John Henrik Clarke, the conflict involves a character against society. Based on your own experience or your knowledge of a period of history, write a short story in which the main character is in conflict with society. Be sure that your story gives enough clues to setting so that readers understand the conflict involved.

Optional Activity At the end of this story, Aaron and his principal experience personal victory. Have you ever achieved something that someone had said you could not achieve? What feelings did you experience? Write a short story based on your experience.

INTRODUCTION
Raymond's Run

Toni Cade Bambara was born in 1939 in New York City and currently lives in Atlanta, Georgia. After graduating from Queens College of the City University of New York, she pursued further studies in both the United States and Europe. Although she worked for several years in social service programs, Bambara's talents eventually directed her into a career of writing and teaching at several well-known universities, among them Rutgers, Duke, and Emory. Her interest in issues affecting African American women is reflected in the many essays, reviews, and stories that she has contributed to magazines and anthologies. Bambara's writing reflects her dedication to African American communities throughout the nation. It is in these communities that she can often be found lecturing and reading from her books.

The following story, taken from the collection *Gorilla, My Love*, reflects the author's belief in the importance of self, family, friends, and neighborhood.

Raymond's Run

by Toni Cade Bambara

◆
◆ I don't have much work to do around the house like some girls. My mother does that. And I don't have to earn my pocket money by hustling; George runs errands for the big boys and sells Christmas cards. And anything else that's got to get done, my father does. All I have to do in life is mind my brother Raymond, which is enough.

Sometimes I slip and say my little brother Raymond. But as any fool can see he's much bigger and he's older too. But a lot of people call him my little brother cause he needs looking after cause he's not quite right. And a lot of smart mouths got lots to say about that too, especially when George was minding him. But now, if anybody has anything to say to Raymond, anything to say about his big head, they have to come by me. And I don't play the dozens[1] or believe in standing around with somebody in my face doing a lot of talking. I much rather just knock you down and take my chances even if I am a little girl with skinny arms and a squeaky voice, which is how I got the name Squeaky. And if things get too rough, I run. And as anybody can tell you, I'm the fastest thing on two feet.

---

1. **the dozens** (DUHZ-uhnz) *n. pl.* (slang) a form of verbal play in which the players exchange taunts and insults

There is no track meet that I don't win the first place medal. I used to win the twenty-yard dash when I was a little kid in kindergarten. Nowadays, it's the fifty-yard dash. And tomorrow I'm subject to run the quarter-meter relay all by myself and come in first, second, and third. The big kids call me Mercury[2] cause I'm the swiftest thing in the neighborhood. Everybody knows that—except two people who know better, my father and me. He can beat me to Amsterdam Avenue with me having a two fire-hydrant headstart and him running with his hands in his pockets whistling. But that's private information. Cause can you imagine some thirty-five-year-old man stuffing himself into PAL shorts to race little kids? So as far as everyone's concerned, I'm the fastest and that goes for Gretchen, too, who has put out the tale that she is going to win the first-place medal this year. Ridiculous. In the second place, she's got short legs. In the third place, she's got freckles. In the first place, no one can beat me and that's all there is to it.

I'm standing on the corner admiring the weather and about to take a stroll down Broadway so I can practice my breathing exercises, and I've got Raymond walking on the inside close to the buildings, cause he's subject to fits of fantasy and starts thinking he's a circus performer and that the curb is a tightrope strung high in the air. And sometimes after a rain he likes to step down off his tightrope right into the gutter and slosh around getting his shoes and cuffs wet. Then I get hit when I get home. Or sometimes if you don't watch him he'll dash across traffic to the island in the middle of Broadway and give the pigeons a fit. Then I have to go behind him apologizing to all the old people sitting around trying to get some sun and getting all upset with the pigeons fluttering around them, scattering their newspapers and upsetting the waxpaper lunches in their laps. So I keep Raymond on the

---

2. Mercury (MER-kyoo-ree) in Roman mythology, the messenger of the gods

inside of me, and he plays like he's driving a stage coach which is O.K. by me so long as he doesn't run me over or interrupt my breathing exercises, which I have to do on account of I'm serious about my running, and I don't care who knows it.

Now, some people like to act like things come easy to them, won't let on that they practice. Not me. I'll highprance down 34th Street like a rodeo pony to keep my knees strong even if it does get my mother uptight so that she walks ahead of me like she's not with me, don't know me, is all by herself on a shopping trip, and I am somebody else's crazy child. Now you take Cynthia Procter for instance. She's just the opposite. If there's a test tomorrow, she'll say something like, "Oh, I guess I'll play handball this afternoon and watch television tonight," just to let you know she ain't thinking about the test. Or like last week when she won the spelling bee for the millionth time, "A good thing you got `receive,' Squeaky, cause I would have got it wrong. I completely forgot about the spelling bee." And she'll clutch the lace on her blouse like it was a narrow escape. Oh, brother. But of course when I pass her house on my early morning trots around the block, she is practicing the scales on the piano over and over and over and over. Then in music class she always lets herself get bumped around so she falls accidently on purpose onto the piano stool and is so surprised to find herself sitting there that she decides just for fun to try out the ole keys. And what do you know—Chopin's[3] waltzes just spring out of her fingertips and she's the most surprised thing in the world. A regular prodigy.[4] I could kill people like that. I stay up all night studying the words for the spelling bee. And you can see me any time of day practicing running. I

---

3. **Chopin** (shoh-PAN) Frédéric Chopin, a famous Polish composer and pianist who lived from 1810 to 1849
4. **prodigy** (PRAHD-uh-jee) *n.* a child of highly unusual talent or genius

never walk if I can trot, and shame on Raymond if he can't keep up. But of course he does, cause if he hangs back someone's liable to walk up to him and get smart, or take his allowance from him, or ask him where he got that great big pumpkin head. People are so stupid sometimes.

So I'm strolling down Broadway breathing out and breathing in on counts of seven, which is my lucky number, and here comes Gretchen and her sidekicks: Mary Louise, who used to be a friend of mine when she first moved to Harlem from Baltimore and got beat up by everybody till I took up for her on account of her mother and my mother used to sing in the same choir when they were young girls, but people ain't grateful, so now she hangs out with the new girl Gretchen and talks about me like a dog; and Rosie, who is as fat as I am skinny and has a big mouth where Raymond is concerned and is too stupid to know that there is not a big deal of difference between herself and Raymond and that she can't afford to throw stones. So they are steady coming up Broadway and I see right away that it's going to be one of those Dodge City[5] scenes cause the street ain't that big and they're close to the buildings just as we are. First I think I'll step into the candy store and look over the new comics and let them pass. But that's chicken and I've got a reputation to consider. So then I think I'll just walk straight on through them or even over them if necessary. But as they get to me, they slow down. I'm ready to fight, cause like I said I don't feature a whole lot of chit-chat, I much prefer to just knock you down right from the jump and save everybody a lotta precious time.

"You signing up for the May Day races?" smiles Mary Louise, only it's not a smile at all. A dumb question like that doesn't deserve an answer. Besides, there's just me

---

5. **Dodge City** (DAHDJ CIH-tee) a city in southwest Kansas that in the late 1800s earned a reputation for being wild and rowdy

and Gretchen standing there really, so no use wasting my breath talking to shadows.

"I don't think you're going to win this time," says Rosie, trying to signify with her hands on her hips all salty, completely forgetting that I have whupped her behind many times for less salt than that.

"I always win cause I'm the best," I say straight at Gretchen who is, as far as I'm concerned, the only one talking in this ventriloquist-dummy routine. Gretchen smiles, but it's not a smile, and I'm thinking that girls never really smile at each other because they don't know how and don't want to know how and there's probably no one to teach us how, cause grown-up girls don't know either. Then they all look at Raymond who has just brought his mule team to a standstill. And they're about to see what trouble they can get into through him.

"What grade you in now, Raymond?"

"You got anything to say to my brother, you say it to me, Mary Louise Williams of Raggedy Town, Baltimore."

"What are you, his mother?" sasses Rosie.

"That's right, Fatso. And the next word out of anybody and I'll be *their* mother too." So they just stand there and Gretchen shifts from one leg to the other and so do they. Then Gretchen puts her hands on her hips and is about to say something with her freckle-face self but doesn't. Then she walks around me looking me up and down but keeps walking up Broadway, and her sidekicks follow her. So me and Raymond smile at each other and he says, "Gidyap" to his team and I continue with my breathing exercises, strolling down Broadway toward the ice man on 145th with not a care in the world cause I am Miss Quicksilver herself.

I take my time getting to the park on May Day because the track meet is the last thing on the program. The biggest thing on the program is the May Pole[6] dancing,

---

6. **May Pole** a high pole, wreathed with flowers or streamers, around which merrymakers dance on the first of May

which I can do without, thank you, even if my mother thinks it's a shame I don't take part and act like a girl for a change. You'd think my mother'd be grateful not to have to make me a white organdy dress with a big satin sash and buy me new white baby-doll shoes that can't be taken out of the box till the big day. You'd think she'd be glad her daughter ain't out there prancing around a May Pole getting the new clothes all dirty and sweaty and trying to act like a fairy or a flower or whatever you're supposed to be when you should be trying to be yourself, whatever that is, which is, as far as I am concerned, a poor Black girl who really can't afford to buy shoes and a new dress you only wear once a lifetime cause it won't fit next year.

I was once a strawberry in a Hansel and Gretel pageant when I was in nursery school and didn't have no better sense than to dance on tiptoe with my arms in a circle over my head doing umbrella steps and being a perfect fool just so my mother and father could come dressed up and clap. You'd think they'd know better than to encourage that kind of nonsense. I am not a strawberry. I do not dance on my toes. I run. That is what I am all about. So I always come late to the May Day program, just in time to get my number pinned on and lay in the grass till they announce the fifty-yard dash.

I put Raymond in the little swings, which is a tight squeeze this year and will be impossible next year. Then I look around for Mr. Pearson, who pins the numbers on. I'm really looking for Gretchen if you want to know the truth, but she's not around. The park is jam-packed. Parents in hats and corsages and breast-pocket handkerchiefs peeking up. Kids in white dresses and light-blue suits. The parkees unfolding chairs and chasing the rowdy kids from Lenox as if they had no right to be there. The big guys with their caps on backwards, leaning against the fence swirling the basketballs on the tips of their fingers, waiting for all these crazy people to clear out the park so they can play. Most of the kids in my class are carrying bass drums and glockenspiels and flutes. You'd think they'd put in a few bongos or something for real like that.

Then here comes Mr. Pearson with his clipboard and his cards and pencils and whistles and safety pins and fifty million other things he's always dropping all over the place with his clumsy self. He sticks out in a crowd because he's on stilts. We used to call him Jack and the Beanstalk to get him mad. But I'm the only one that can outrun him and get away, and I'm too grown for that silliness now.

"Well, Squeaky," he says, checking my name off the list and handing me number seven and two pins. And I'm thinking he's got no right to call me Squeaky, if I can't call him Beanstalk.

"Hazel Elizabeth Deborah Parker," I correct him and tell him to write it down on his board.

"Well, Hazel Elizabeth Deborah Parker, going to give someone else a break this year?" I squint at him real hard to see if he is seriously thinking I should lose the race on purpose just to give someone else a break. "Only six girls running this time," he continues, shaking his head sadly like it's my fault all of New York didn't turn out in sneakers. "That new girl should give you a run for your money." He looks around the park for Gretchen like a periscope in a submarine movie. "Wouldn't it be a nice gesture if you were . . . to ahhh . . . "

I give him such a look he couldn't finish putting that idea into words. Grownups got a lot of nerve sometimes. I pin number seven to myself and stomp away, I'm so burnt. And I go straight for the track and stretch out on the grass while the band winds up with "Oh, the Monkey Wrapped His Tail Around the Flag Pole," which my teacher calls by some other name. The man on the loudspeaker is calling everyone over to the track and I'm on my back looking at the sky, trying to pretend I'm in the country, but I can't, because even grass in the city feels hard as sidewalk, and there's just no pretending you are anywhere but in a "concrete jungle" as my grandfather says.

The twenty-yard dash takes all of two minutes cause most of the little kids don't know no better than to run off the track or run the wrong way or run smack into the fence and fall down and cry. One little kid, though, has got the good sense to run straight for the white ribbon up ahead so he wins. Then the second-graders line up for the thirty-yard dash and I don't even bother to turn my head to watch cause Raphael Perez always wins. He wins before he even begins by psyching the runners, telling them they're going to trip on their shoelaces and fall on their faces or lose their shorts or something, which he doesn't really have to do since he is very fast, almost as fast as I am. After that is the forty-yard dash which I used to run when I was in first grade. Raymond is hollering from the swings cause he knows I'm about to do my thing cause the man on the loudspeaker has just announced the fifty-yard dash, although he might just as well be giving a recipe for angel food cake cause you can hardly make out what he's sayin for the static. I get up and slip off my sweat pants and then I see Gretchen standing at the starting line, kicking her legs out like a pro. Then as I get into place I see that ole Raymond is on line on the other side of the fence, bending down with his fingers on the ground just like he knew what he was doing. I was going to yell at him but then I didn't. It burns up your energy to holler.

Every time, just before I take off in a race, I always feel like I'm in a dream, the kind of dream you have when you're sick with fever and feel all hot and weightless. I dream I'm flying over a sandy beach in the early morning sun, kissing the leaves of the trees as I fly by. And there's always the smell of apples, just like in the country when I was little and used to think I was a choo-choo train, running through the fields of corn and chugging up the hill to the orchard. And all the time I'm dreaming this, I get lighter and lighter until I'm flying over the beach again, getting blown through the sky like a feather that weighs nothing at all. But once I spread my fingers in the dirt and crouch over the Get on Your Mark, the dream goes and I am solid again and am telling myself, Squeaky you must win, you must win, you are the fastest thing in the world, you can even beat your father up Amsterdam if you really try. And then I feel my weight coming back just behind my knees then down to my feet then into the earth and the pistol shot explodes in my blood and I am off and weightless again, flying past the other runners, my arms pumping up and down and the whole world is quiet except for the crunch as I zoom over gravel in the track. I glance to my left and there is no one there. To the right, a blurred Gretchen, who's got her chin jutting out as if it would win the race all by itself. And on the other side of the fence is Raymond with his arms down to his side and the palms tucked up behind him, running in his very own style, and it's the first time I ever say that and I almost stop to watch my brother Raymond on his first run. But the white ribbon is bouncing toward me and I tear past it, racing into the distance till my feet with a mind of their own start digging up footfuls of dirt and brake me short. Then all the kids standing on the side pile on me, banging me on the back slapping my head with their May Day programs, for I have won again and everybody on 151st Street can walk tall for another year.

"In first place . . ." the man on the loudspeaker starts to whine. Then static. And I lean down to catch my breath and here comes Gretchen walking back, for she's overshot the finish line too, huffing and puffing with her hands on her hips taking it slow, breathing in steady time like a real pro and I sort of like her a little for the first time. "In first place . . ." and then three or four voices get all mixed up on the loudspeaker and I dig my sneaker into the grass and stare at Gretchen who's staring back, we both wondering just who did win. I can hear old Beanstalk arguing with the man on the loudspeaker and then a few others running their mouths about what the stopwatches say. Then I hear Raymond yanking at the fence to call me and I wave to shush him, but he keeps rattling the fence like a gorilla in a cage like in them gorilla movies, but then like a dancer or something he starts climbing up nice and easy but very fast. And it occurs to me, watching how smoothly he climbs hand over hand and remembering how he looked running with his arms down to his side and with the wind pulling his mouth back and his teeth showing and all, it occurred to me that Raymond would make a very fine runner. Doesn't he always keep up with me on my trots? And he surely knows how to breathe in counts of seven cause he's always doing it at the dinner table, which drives my brother George up the wall. And I'm smiling to beat the band cause if I've lost this race, or if me and Gretchen tied, or even if I've won, I can always retire as a runner and begin a whole new career as a coach with Raymond as my champion. After all, with a little more study I can beat Cynthia and her phony self at the spelling bee. And if I bugged my mother, I could get piano lessons and become a star. And I have a big rep as the baddest thing around. And I've got a roomful of ribbons and awards. But what has Raymond got to call his own?

So I stand there with my new plans, laughing out loud by this time as Raymond jumps down from the fence and runs over with his teeth showing and his arms down to the side, which no one before him has quite mastered as a running style. And by the time he comes over I'm jumping up and down so glad to see him—my brother Raymond, a great runner in the family tradition. But of course everyone thinks I'm jumping up and down because the men on the loudspeaker have finally gotten themselves together and compared notes and are announcing "In first place—Miss Hazel Elizabeth Deborah Parker." (Dig that.)

"In second place—Miss Gretchen P. Lewis." And I look over at Gretchen wondering what the "P" stands for. And I smile. Cause she's good, no doubt about it. Maybe she'd like to help me coach Raymond; she obviously is serious about running, as any fool can see. And she nods to congratulate me and then she smiles. And I smile. We stand there with this big smile of respect between us. It's about as real a smile as girls can do for each other, considering we don't practice real smiling every day, you know, cause maybe we too busy being flowers or fairies or strawberries instead of something honest and worthy of respect . . . you know . . . like being people.

AFTER YOU READ

Exchanging Backgrounds and Cultures

1. How does this story reflect the importance of family, a theme common in African American literature?

2. What strengths of character does the author give Hazel Elizabeth Deborah Parker?

3. When Squeaky refers to herself as "a poor Black girl," do you think she is feeling sorry for herself? Explain.

What Do You Think?

Which part of the story helped you to see people—or even yourself—in a new way? What new understanding did you gain?

Experiencing Fiction

Sometimes people try to feel superior by making others feel inferior, as the girls did when they taunted Raymond. Have you ever found yourself in a situation similar to Squeaky's? What were your feelings? Write a short scene in which the main character defends himself or herself, or a friend. Try writing the scene in the first person, as Toni Cade Bambara did. Remember that when writing first-person narrative, the main character doesn't know the thoughts of the other characters.

Optional Activity Difficult situations—such as having a disabled brother or sister—sometimes make people stronger. Think of a difficult situation in your life or in the life of someone you know well. Based on your experience or knowledge, try writing a short fictional scene in which you explore the effect that the situation has on the character involved.

INTRODUCTION

Roll of Thunder,
Hear My Cry

Mildred D. Taylor was born in Jackson, Mississippi, in 1943 and grew up in Toledo, Ohio. After completing her college education at the University of Toledo, Taylor joined the Peace Corps and taught history and English in Ethiopia. During the 1960s, Taylor pursued a master's degree in English at the University of Colorado, where she helped found the Black Student Alliance and worked to establish a Black Studies department.

As a writer, Taylor's greatest inspiration has come from her father. Throughout her childhood, she listened to his stories about African Americans who were proud of their culture and history. Taylor captures the spirit and strength of these people in her characters. Her series of six novels traces the lives of the Logan family from the Great Depression through the Civil Rights Movement.

The selection you are about to read is from Taylor's second novel *Roll of Thunder, Hear My Cry*. In this episode, Mary Logan defies white members of the Board of Education and teaches her students about the cruelty of slavery.

from *Roll of Thunder, Hear My Cry*

by Mildred D. Taylor

 . . . "Cassie Logan!"

"Yes'm, Miz Crocker?"

"That's the third time I've caught you daydreaming this morning. Just because you managed to come in first on the examinations last week doesn't mean a thing this week. We're in a new quarter and everyone's slate is clean. You'll make no A's by daydreaming. You understand that?"

"Yes'm," I said, not bothering to add that she repeated herself so much that all a body had to do was listen to the first few minutes of her lesson to be free to daydream to her heart's content.

"I think you'd just better sit in the back where you're not so comfortable," she said. "Then maybe you'll pay more attention."

"But—"

Miss Crocker raised her hand, indicating that she did not want to hear another word, and banished me to the very last row in front of the window. I slid onto the cold seat after its former occupant had eagerly left it for my warm quarters by the stove. As soon as Miss Crocker turned away, I mumbled a few indignant phrases, then hugged my Christmas sweater to me. I tried to pay attention to Miss Crocker but the cold creeping under the windowsill made it impossible. Unable to bear the draft, I decided to line the sill with paper from my notebook. I ripped out the paper, then turned to the window. As I did, a man passed under it and disappeared.

The man was Kaleb[1] Wallace.

I raised my hand. "Uh, Miz Crocker, may I be excused please, ma'am? I gotta . . . well, you know. . . ."

As soon as I had escaped Miss Crocker, I dashed to the front of the building. Kaleb Wallace was standing in front of the seventh-grade-class building talking to Mr. Wellever and two white men whom I couldn't make out from where I stood. When the men entered the building, I turned and sped to the rear and carefully climbed onto the woodpile stacked behind it. I peeked cautiously through a broken window into Mama's classroom. The men were just entering, Kaleb Wallace first, followed by a man I didn't know and Mr. Harlan Granger.

Mama seemed startled to see the men, but when Mr. Granger said, "Been hearing 'bout your teaching, Mary, so as members of the school board we thought we'd come by and learn something," she merely nodded and went on with her lesson. Mr. Wellever left the room, returning shortly with three folding chairs for the visitors; he himself remained standing.

Mama was in the middle of history and I knew that was bad. I could tell Stacey knew it too; he sat tense near the back of the room, his lips very tight, his eyes on the men. But Mama did not flinch; she always started her history class the first thing in the morning when the students were most alert, and I knew that the hour was not yet up. To make matters worse, her lesson for the day was slavery. She spoke on the cruelty of it; of the rich

---

1. **Kaleb** (KAY-luhb)

economic cycle it generated as slaves produced the raw products for the factories of the North and Europe; how the country profited and grew from the free labor of a people still not free.

Before she had finished, Mr. Granger picked up a student's book, flipped it open to the pasted-over front cover, and pursed his lips. "Thought these books belonged to the county," he said, interrupting her. Mama glanced over at him, but did not reply. Mr. Granger turned the pages, stopped, and read something. "I don't see all them things you're teaching in here."

"That's because they're not in there," Mama said.

"Well, if it ain't in here, then you got no right teaching it. This book's approved by the Board of Education and you're expected to teach what's in it."

"I can't do that."

"And why not?"

Mama, her back straight and her eyes fixed on the men, answered, "Because all that's in that book isn't true."

Mr. Granger stood. He laid the book back on the student's desk and headed for the door. The other board member and Kaleb Wallace followed. At the door Mr. Granger stopped and pointed at Mama. "You must be some kind of smart, Mary, to know more than the fellow who wrote that book. Smarter than the school board, too, I reckon."

Mama remained silent, and Mr. Wellever gave her no support.

"In fact," Mr. Granger continued, putting on his hat, "you so smart I expect you'd best just forget about teaching altogether . . . then thataway you'll have plenty of time to write your own book." With that he turned his back on her, glanced at Mr. Wellever to make sure his meaning was clear, and left with the others behind him.

We waited for Mama after school was out. Stacey had sent T.J. and Claude on, and the four of us, silent and patient, were sitting on the steps when Mama emerged. She smiled down at us, seemingly not surprised that we were there.

I looked up at her, but I couldn't speak. I had never really thought much about Mama's teaching before; that was just a part of her being Mama. But now that she could not teach, I felt resentful and angry, and I hated Mr. Granger.

"You all know?" she asked. We nodded as she slowly descended the stairs. Stacey took one handle of her heavy black satchel[2] and I took the other. Christopher-John and Little Man each took one of her hands, and we started across the lawn.

"M-Mama," said Christopher-John when we reached the road, "can't you ever teach no more?"

Mama did not answer immediately. When she did, her voice was muffled. "Somewhere else maybe, but not here—at least not for a while."

"But how's come, Mama?" demanded Little Man. "How's come?"

Mama bit into her lower lip and gazed at the road. "Because, baby," she said finally, "I taught things some folks just didn't want to hear."

When we reached home, Papa and Mr. Morrison were both in the kitchen with Big Ma[3] drinking coffee. As we entered, Papa searched our faces. His eyes settled on Mama; the pain was in her face. "What's wrong?" he asked.

Mama sat down beside him. She pushed back a strand of hair that had worked its way free of the chignon,[4] but it

---

2. **satchel** (SACH-uhl) *n.* a small bag for carrying clothes, books, or other small objects
3. **Big Ma** the children's name for their grandmother
4. **chignon** (SHEEN-yahn) *n.* a hairstyle in which the hair is gathered into a coil at the back of the neck

fell back into her face again and she left it there. "I got fired."

Big Ma put down her cup weakly without a word.

Papa reached out and touched Mama. She said, "Harlan Granger came to the school with Kaleb Wallace and one of the school-board members. Somebody had told them about those books I'd pasted over . . . but that was only an excuse. They're just getting at us any way they can because of shopping in Vicksburg."[5] Her voice cracked. "What'll we do, David? We needed that job."

Papa gently pushed the stray hair back over her ear. "We'll get by. . . . Plant more cotton maybe. But we'll get by." There was quiet reassurance in his voice.

Mama nodded and stood.

"Where you goin', child?" Big Ma asked.

"Outside. I want to walk for a bit."

Christopher-John, Little Man, and I turned to follow her, but Papa called us back. "Leave your mama be," he said.

As we watched her slowly cross the backyard to the barren garden and head toward the south pasture, Mr. Morrison said, "You know with you here, Mr. Logan, you got no need of me. Maybe there's work to be had around here. . . . Maybe I could get something . . . help you out."

Papa stared across at Mr. Morrison. "There's no call for you to do that," he said. "I'm not paying you anything as it is."

Mr. Morrison said softly, "I got me a nice house to live in, the best cooking a man could want, and for the first time in a long time I got me a family. That's right good pay, I'd say."

Papa nodded. "You're a good man, Mr. Morrison, and

---

5. **shopping in Vicksburg** The family has not shopped at the local store because the store owner treats African Americans unfairly.

I thank you for the offer, but I'll be leaving in a few weeks and I'd rather you was here." His eyes focused on Mama again, a tiny figure in the distance now.

"Papa," rasped Christopher-John, moving close to him, "M-Mama gonna be all right?"

Papa turned and, putting his arms around Christopher-John, drew him even nearer. "Son, your mama . . . she's born to teaching like the sun is born to shine. And it's gonna be hard on her not teaching anymore. It's gonna be real hard 'cause ever since she was a wee bitty girl down in the Delta[6] she wanted to be a teacher."

"And Grandpa wanted her to be one, too, didn't he, Papa?" said Christopher-John.

Papa nodded. "Your mama was his baby child and every penny he'd get his hands on he'd put it aside for her schooling . . . and that wasn't easy for him either 'cause he was a tenant farmer[7] and he didn't see much cash money. But he'd promised your grandmama 'fore she died to see that your mama got an education, and when your mama 'come high-school age, he sent her up to Jackson to school, then on to teacher training school. It was just 'cause he died her last year of schooling that she come on up here to teach 'stead of going back to the Delta."

"And y'all got married and she ain't gone back down there no more," interjected Little Man.

Papa smiled faintly at Little Man and stood up. "That's right, son. She was too smart and pretty to let get away." He stooped and looked out the window again, then back at us. "She's a strong, fine woman, your mama, and this thing won't keep her down . . . but it's hurt her bad. So I want

---

6. **the Delta** the place where the Mississippi River meets the Gulf of Mexico

7. **tenant farmer** a person who farms land owned by someone else and pays rent by giving the landowner cash or a share of the crops

y'all to be extra thoughtful for the next few days—and remember what I told you, you hear?"

"Yessir, Papa," we answered.

Papa left us then and went onto the back porch. There he leaned against the porch pillar for several minutes staring out toward the pasture; but after a while he stepped into the yard and crossed the garden to join Mama. . . .

AFTER YOU READ

Exchanging Backgrounds and Cultures

1. What does Mary Logan teach her students about slavery? Why does this anger the school board?
2. What is Cassie's reaction when she discovers that her mother has been fired?
3. How does this selection reflect the pride and strength of the Logan family?

What Do You Think?

Which character did you like best? Which did you like least? Why?

Experiencing Fiction

Like real people, fictional characters must often make difficult decisions. They must also face the consequences—both good and bad—of those decisions. In *Roll of Thunder, Hear My Cry*, Mary Logan decides to teach her students about the injustices of slavery and, as a result, is fired from her job. Imagine that she decides instead to teach the lesson in the textbook. What might have been the consequences of this decision? How might Mary have felt afterward? How might the Logan family have reacted? Write a short scene that depicts this situation. Try writing the scene from the point of view of a specific character, such as Cassie, Stacey, David Logan, or Mary Logan herself.

Optional Activity Assume the personality of Cassie. Write a journal entry in which she reflects on the incident involving her mother and the school board.

INTRODUCTION

This Strange New Feeling

Julius Lester was born in 1939 in St. Louis, Missouri, and spent his childhood in Kansas City, Kansas. Sheltered within a supportive African American community, young Julius had no direct contact with prejudice until he visited his grandmother in Pine Bluff, Arkansas. There, he felt confused by the "No Colored Allowed" signs that implied he was not good enough. Despite that experience, he says that he grew up with a strong sense of self, thanks to his childhood home.

Like many other young African Americans, Lester responded to the call for black power in the 1960s. His beliefs are reflected in many of his writings. Since 1971, he has been a professor at the University of Massachusetts, Amherst.

The selection you are about to read is taken from Lester's collection of stories about newly freed slaves, called *This Strange New Feeling*. In this episode, an old African American slave named Isaac, relying on his instinct about people, makes a daring request of a white planter.

from *This Strange New Feeling*

by Julius Lester

TWO

1

◇
◇ Thomas McMahon was a fat, bald white man who sweated profusely, summer and winter. Uncle Isaac had never seen him when he wasn't mopping his round, slick head with a big red handkerchief and breathing noisily, as if he had just finished running five miles. Now that would have been a sight!

Yet of all the white men Uncle Isaac knew, Thomas McMahon was the one. It was more than a feeling Uncle Isaac had about him, though the feeling was important. McMahon was the only white man in that part of Maryland who didn't own slaves. Uncle Isaac guessed that he still had about a hundred acres left from all he'd sold over the years, and he could've been a rich man if he had owned slaves. Yet except for the few acres he planted in tobacco, vegetables, and hay, his land was overgrown with trees and underbrush. And God was perhaps the only one who remembered the last time his house had been painted. The barn was beginning to lean as if there were a constant wind blowing against it. He was a strange man, but he was the one.

Almost absentmindedly Isaac ran the tip of his forefinger over his thumbnail. It was as hard and thick as the blade of a plow, but it was the mind behind the nail that made the difference. It took a man like Uncle Isaac, who knew tobacco better than he knew himself, to look at a tobacco plant and know precisely where to cut the top with his thumbnail. That was what made the tobacco grow large, sometimes seven feet high with leaves six feet long.

Uncle Isaac had heard white men offer Master Lindsay $2,000 for him. That was a lot of money for an old slave who did no heavy work. But Master Lindsay wouldn't think of selling him. Isaac was allowed to hire himself out, though, to the other planters. However, he had to give half of what he earned to Master Lindsay. Uncle Isaac supposed if Jessie was still alive, he would've spent the money and bought chairs, a table, clothes, and food. But caring about such things died when she died. He kept the money in a sack that he hid behind loose bricks in the fireplace.

As Uncle Isaac made his way through the woods that Sunday afternoon, he didn't think what he would do if Mr. McMahon turned him down. There wasn't another white he'd dare present such an idea to, not if he cared about his life. But when he remembered all the years he had used his thick thumbnail on Mr. McMahon's tobacco, and how he always invited Isaac to sit in the shade of the porch and drink a big glass of lemonade and then talk all afternoon, Isaac knew. Thomas McMahon was the one.

When McMahon looked up from the shade of the porch where he sat in his rocking chair and saw Isaac walk out of the woods, he wondered how old Isaac was. He looked as old and eternal as God, with the big white beard like clouds around his black face. But he walked as easily as any young man, and certainly more nimbly than McMahon had ever walked. Isaac had to be eighty if he was a day. Any slave who lived that long was not only strong but wise in the ways of a wicked and hard world. And that made Thomas wonder why Isaac was coming to see him on a Sunday afternoon.

"Afternoon, Mr. McMahon," Isaac said easily as he crossed the dusty yard the chickens had picked clean of grass.

"Howdy, Isaac," McMahon returned in his high-pitched nasal voice, which reminded Isaac of a weak train whistle.

Uncle Isaac stopped at the edge of the porch and the two men stared at each other for a moment. Thomas mopped his head with the big red handkerchief and looked into the dark eyes imbedded in the black face. He shifted uncomfortably, knowing it was insolent[1] for a black to stare him in the eye like that. For an instant McMahon wished he was the kind of white man who would've knocked Isaac down for looking anywhere else except at the ground.

"It's strange to see you over here, Isaac," he said coolly. "You took care of my tobacco a while back, as I recall."

"Yes, sir," Isaac returned evenly.

McMahon couldn't withstand Isaac's stare any longer, and he wiped his face with the big handkerchief to escape from those eyes. "What can I do for you?"

"Nothing for me, sir." Isaac smiled.

McMahon wanted to be annoyed. Why didn't Isaac just say what he wanted? But that wasn't his way. He made you come to him, and despite himself Thomas McMahon knew he would.

"Mind if I set down here on the steps, sir, and rest these old bones?"

"Sit if you want to," Thomas returned gruffly.

Isaac sat down, his back to the fat man in the rocking chair. "Your tobacco turned out right well."

---

1. **insolent** (IHN-suh-luhnt) *adj.* deliberately rude

"Can't complain."

"Right well," Isaac repeated. "You plant about four acres, don't you, sir?"

"You know that as well as I do."

Isaac ignored the ragged edge of annoyance in McMahon's voice. He nodded slowly, and then turned and stared directly into the white man's eyes. "I always thought it was strange that a man with as much land as you own wouldn't plant thirty, forty acres of tobacco." His voice was no longer casual, and his statement sounded like a challenge and rebuke.

"I do all right," McMahon managed to say, startled by the abrupt change in the conversation. "What business is it of yours?"

Isaac smiled and turned back to stare over the field where the tobacco was growing. "It must've hurt you mighty bad when you had to sell off another twenty acres last year."

McMahon's face turned even redder than its normal strawberry color. "What's it to you?"

"When you sold that land, I thought you was going to buy you some slaves for sure this time, and plant the hundred acres you got left in tobacco so you could earn some money to do you some good."

"You got some slaves you want to sell, Isaac?" McMahon asked sarcastically.

Isaac laughed. "Now wouldn't that be something? A black man with slaves to sell." He laughed loudly, and just when McMahon began his tittering wheezy laugh, Isaac turned his whole body around and said firmly, "I got a slave I want to free."

McMahon felt his jaw drop, and the sweat slid off his head and down his face. "Are you crazy?" he gasped, wiping his face and neck nervously. "I could have you whipped to within an inch of your life if I told Lindsay what you just said."

"But you wouldn't," Uncle Isaac said with quiet confidence. "Not if I know anything about people."

"What—what do you mean?" Thomas McMahon asked, unable to hide his curiosity, believing in spite of himself that this old black man was about to answer for him the riddle his life had been.

"It took me a while to understand it, Mr. McMahon," Isaac said conversationally. "I'd think about you with almost two hundred acres of rich land, good land. And I've watched you sell off half of it over the years. And it didn't make sense. I'd say to myself, 'Now here's a white man who could be one of the richest slave owners in the state of Maryland. But he scarcely lives better than poor white trash.' So I asked myself, 'Why would a man who could be rich deprive himself?'"

"Well, you know so much. What's the answer?" McMahon asked, with obvious forced anger.

Isaac smiled softly. "Because he can't bring himself to do what other men do to make themselves rich."

"Maybe," Thomas allowed after a long pause. "Maybe," he repeated, adding hurriedly, "But that don't mean I'm a fool! I don't know what you have schemed up, but let me tell you this. I don't plan on going to jail for helping a slave get free. And that's final!"

Isaac erupted into a big laugh. "Jail? Who's talking about jail, Mr. McMahon? I'm talking about New York."

Thomas stared at Isaac for a moment, and when he understood, a smile spread slowly across his chubby red face. He wiped his head and chuckled. "Isaac, if you weren't so old and decrepit, I'd take a horsewhip to you for putting ideas in the head of an old, fat white man who's never done much with his life." He laughed. "You think it'll work?"

"I know it will, sir. I know it will."

The two men laughed until tears streamed down their faces, and then they laughed some more.

2

It was the last Sunday in September when Thomas McMahon gave a low whistle and the two horses jerked into motion, pulling the wagon filled with bales of tobacco. The sun was showing orange over the horizon as Thomas began his annual trip to New York to sell his tobacco.

In past years he had dreaded this trip, necessitated by the dislike the other planters and poor whites had for a man who had freed the slaves he had inherited from his father. If he had known then how long they would refuse to do business with him, he might have kept the slaves. Forty years had passed, but they hadn't forgotten.

As a young man of twenty-two he'd only wanted to do the right thing. But what had been right for those blacks had been a disaster for his own life. He supposed he could've sold the plantation and moved North, but McMahons were known for being stubborn. So he'd stayed and gotten so fat he could scarcely fit into a rocking chair. It was as if he had been punishing himself for being different. Two hundred eighty pounds of blubber sitting on the porch and watching the weeds grow.

Yet an old black man, as ancient as the Big Dipper and as wise as the earth that knew how to turn a tiny seed into a seven-foot-high tobacco plant, had seen something worthwhile in him.

When he got back, he would ask Isaac how he had managed to see beneath all the fat and know that Thomas McMahon hated slavery. Thomas had always believed that he'd freed his father's slaves because he was too lazy to run a plantation. But he knew now that he hadn't wanted to remember how his father had made him watch slaves whipped, or the light-skinned children who were his half-brothers and -sisters, though no one said so, or the day his father had taken him to slave auctions to teach him to judge "nigger flesh." Thomas hadn't wanted to remember, so he'd convinced himself that he was too lazy and set the thirty slaves free.

This Sunday morning it was thirty-one. Thomas chuckled as he thought about the tobacco tied in bales in the wagon behind him. Even if he told someone, they wouldn't believe that at the bottom of the wagon, wrapped inside a bale of cured tobacco leaves, was a young black man whom Isaac called Ras.

3

Ras stared through the window of his room in the white house on Center Street in Calais, Maine, marveling yet again at the snow piled high outside. Two months had passed since the night he had unrolled himself from the tobacco leaves outside the warehouse in New York City, where Thomas McMahon took his tobacco to sell. Only two months. It seemed like a life lived by someone else.

If anyone from that life had seen him now, they would not have recognized the erect man in the dark suit with the cravat[2] at his throat. And if they had asked his name, he would've answered proudly, "Ras McMahon." His landlady called him Mr. McMahon, and only occasionally did he forget that she was speaking to him. Once, while walking along the street, he happened to see a smiling reflection in a store window and walked half a block before realizing that it was him. That's what freedom looked like, he concluded.

The days passed with a leisureliness that was almost mysterious. It was a curious feeling to sleep as long and as

---

2. **cravat** (kruh-VAT) *n.* a necktie

often as he wanted, to eat fish until his stomach ached. With the money Uncle Isaac had given him Ras would not have to work until spring, at least. Calais was a lumbering town, and he knew he could swing an axe as good as any man. Being free now, he thought he could fell a tree with a single swing. Free! It was such a tiny word for something so big. . . .

AFTER YOU READ

Exchanging Backgrounds and Cultures

1. Why was Uncle Isaac's plan of approaching a white planter risky? Why did he choose Thomas McMahon?

2. What personal conflict did Isaac's request create for Thomas McMahon?

3. Despite the social and cultural barriers that existed between them, how do you think Isaac and the white planter felt about each other?

What Do You Think?

How did you react to Thomas McMahon as you read the story? How is he different from your idea of a Southern plantation owner?

Experiencing Fiction

When Uncle Isaac approached Thomas McMahon, he suspected that the planter did not fit the stereotype of the Southern plantation owner. He relied on his own judgment and personal observation of the man. Have you ever formed an opinion about someone, only to change your opinion once you got to know that person? Using your own experience or that of someone you know, write a short story in which the main character reaches a new understanding about someone else. If you write in the third person, as Julius Lester did, you can reveal the thoughts and feelings of any of your characters.

Optional Activity Could this story have happened at another time and another place? Choose a favorite period of history and write a short story in which characters cross social and cultural barriers, as Uncle Isaac and Thomas McMahon did. Be sure that you include enough details to establish the setting of your story.

UNIT 2: FOCUS ON WRITING

Unlike nonfiction, which is factual, fiction features places, events, and people that spring from the author's imagination. However, writers of short stories and novels often draw upon their cultural backgrounds and their own experiences to create believable characters, settings, and situations. In "The Boy Who Painted Christ Black," for instance, John Henrik Clarke draws upon his own experience of growing up in Georgia in the 1920s and 1930s.

Writing a Short Story

Short stories often focus on a single theme, episode, conflict, or character. Write a short story based on an important experience in your life or in the life of an interesting person you have known.

The Writing Process

Good writing requires both time and effort. An effective writer completes a number of stages that together make up the writing process. The stages of the writing process are given below to help guide you through your assignment.

Prewriting

Think about your past. Which memories stand out most clearly? List some of your ideas, then decide which one you might want to explore further. After selecting an idea, set up a chart with columns for each of the story elements: setting, characters, conflict, plot, and theme. Make notes in each column to help you shape your story. You might ask yourself the following questions:

Setting: When and where does the story take place? What words will I use to describe the setting?

Characters: Who will be the main character? What other characters will take part in the action?

Conflict: What is the central problem? Is it internal (within the character's mind) or external (between the character and something or someone else)? In "Raymond's Run," it is external, between Squeaky and the other girls.

Plot: What events will take place? What will be the high point, or climax, of the story? How will the conflict be resolved?

Theme: What is the idea behind the story? How will the story reveal this theme?

Before you begin to write, decide from what point of view the story will be told. There are many ways to do this. In "Raymond's Run," for instance, the main character tells the story herself. "The Boy Who Painted Christ Black" is also a first-person narrative, but the narrator is unknown. Or you could tell the story in the third person, as Julius Lester did, giving you the advantage of knowing everything about your characters.

Drafting and Revising

Refer to your prewriting chart as you write a first draft, but do not feel bound by it. Remember that the first draft is not the final version of the story. Don't forget that it is always more interesting to show readers something rather than telling them; use imagery or descriptive words to make your story more effective.

As you revise your short story—if possible, with the help of a friend—eliminate passages or details that do not seem important to the story. If you have not already done so, choose a title that tells something about the story and attracts a reader's attention.

Proofreading and Publishing

Proofread your short story, and correct any errors in spelling, grammar, punctuation, and capitalization. Make a neat final copy.

Share your story with a friend, or submit it to a school publication. You may also want to ask your teacher about local or national literary contests for young writers.

UNIT 3

POETRY OF THE AFRICAN AMERICANS

When poets write, they often use words in unusual ways to add to the meaning of the poem. This makes reading poetry quite a different experience from reading prose. You may need to read a poem several times to detect all the layers of meaning that the poet has constructed.

Poets use a variety of literary techniques to build meaning. **Imagery** refers to the use of descriptive language to form mental images. A specific kind of imagery that poets use is called **figurative language**, involving figures of speech. Maya Angelou's poem, in which "the Rock cries out to us," relies on **personification.** Personification is a figure of speech in which an object or an idea is given human qualities. Other common figures of speech are **similes**, which compare two objects by using the words *like* or *as,* and **metaphors**, in which one thing is spoken of as though it were something else. Nikki Giovanni uses a metaphor in the phrase "Black love is Black wealth."

Sometimes poets use the sound of words to create an effect. **Repetition**, the repeated use of any element of language, helps to produce rhythm and to link ideas. In Mari Evans's poem, "Who Can Be Born Black," the repeated phrase "come together/in a coming togetherness" creates a distinctive rhythm and helps focus on the central idea. **Alliteration** is the repetition of consonant sounds at the beginnings of words or accented syllables as in Angelou's "wall of the world."

In the first group of poems, the poets draw on the strength of their culture and experiences. In the second group, the poets give a personal view of their world. As you read, be aware of how each poet uses special techniques to add to the meaning and effects of their poems.

Dance has always been an important part of the African American culture. In *Two Dancers*, African American artist Joseph Holston uses fluid lines and contrasting dark and light areas to express rhythm and energy. Notice how the curved arms and legs push out to the very edges of the rectangular frame.

INTRODUCTION

Section 1:
Toward Tomorrow's
Triumphs

The poets in this section acknowledge the difficulties that African Americans have faced, while praising the qualities and values that have enriched their lives—love, determination, and hope. Maya Angelou is one of the best-known African American poets writing today. At the request of President Bill Clinton, Angelou wrote her dramatic poem "On the Pulse of Morning" for his inauguration in January 1993.

Nikki Giovanni became one of the leading African American voices in the late 1960s. An important theme in her poetry has always been love in the African American family. In "Nikki-Rosa" Giovanni draws on her childhood memories.

Abiodun Oyewole's poetry reflects a love for life and an appreciation of the heritage and history of African Americans. "Another Mountain" is a metaphor for his personal struggles and triumphs.

Lucille Clifton, born in New York in 1936, is known for poetry that looks simple yet reflects deep feelings about her heritage, the family, and the struggle to live with dignity. She has twice been nominated for the Pulitzer Prize in poetry.

Nikki-Rosa

by Nikki Giovanni

childhood remembrances are always a drag
if you're Black
you always remember things like living in Woodlawn[1]
with no inside toilet
and if you become famous or something
they never talk about how happy you were to have your
    mother
all to yourself and
how good the water felt when you got your bath from one
    of those
big tubs that folk in chicago barbecue in
and somehow when you talk about home
it never gets across how much you
understood their feelings
as the whole family attended meetings about Hollydale[2]
and even though you remember
your biographers never understand
your father's pain as he sells his stock

---

1. **Woodlawn** a city near Cincinnati, Ohio
2. **Hollydale** an African American community near Cincinnati, Ohio;
   Hollydale was the first settlement in this area to be developed and
   financed solely by African Americans.

and another dream goes
and though you're poor it isn't poverty that
concerns you
and though they fought a lot
it isn't your father's drinking that makes any difference
but only that everybody is together and you
and your sister have happy birthdays and very good
    christmasses
and I really hope no white person ever has cause to write
    about me
because they never understand Black love is Black wealth
    and they'll
probably talk about my hard childhood and never
    understand that
all the while I was quite happy

listen children

by Lucille Clifton

listen children
keep this in the place
you have for keeping
always
keep it all ways

we have never hated black

listen
we have been ashamed
hopeless   tired   mad
but always
all ways
we loved us

we have always loved each other
children   all ways

pass it on

Another Mountain

by Abiodun Oyewole

Sometimes there's a mountain
that I must climb
even after I've climbed one already
But my legs are tired now
and my arms need a rest
my mind is too weary right now
But I must climb before the storm comes
before the earth rocks
and an avalanche of clouds bury me
and smother my soul
And so I prepare myself for another climb
Another Mountain
and I tell myself it is nothing
it is just some more dirt and stone
and every now and then I should reach
another plateau and enjoy the view
of the trees and the flowers below
And I am young enough to climb
and strong enough to make it to any top
You see the wind has warned me
about settling too long
about peace without struggle
The wind has warned me
and taught me how to fly
But my wings only work
After I've climbed a mountain

On the Pulse of Morning

by Maya Angelou

A Rock, A River, A Tree
Hosts to species long since departed,
Marked the mastodon,[1]
The dinosaur, who left dried tokens
Of their sojourn here
On our planet floor,
Any broad alarm of their hastening doom
Is lost in the gloom of dust and ages.

But today, the Rock cries out to us, clearly,
    forcefully,
Come, you may stand upon my
Back and face your distant destiny,
But seek no haven in my shadow.
I will give you no hiding place down here.

You, created only a little lower than
The angels, have crouched too long in
The bruising darkness
Have lain too long
Face down in ignorance.
Your mouths spilling words

Armed for slaughter.
The Rock cries out to us today, you may
    stand upon me,
But do not hide your face.

Across the wall of the world,
A River sings a beautiful song. It says,
Come, rest here by my side.

---

1. mastodon (MAS-tuh-dahn) *n.* a member of an extinct family of mammals related to elephants

Each of you, a bordered country,
Delicate and strangely made proud,
Yet thrusting perpetually under siege.
Your armed struggles for profit
Have left collars of waste upon
My shore, currents of debris upon my breast.
Yet today I call you to my riverside,
If you will study war no more. Come,
Clad in peace, and I will sing the songs
The Creator gave to me when I and the
Tree and the rock were one.
Before cynicism was a bloody sear across your
Brow and when you yet knew you still
Knew nothing.
The River sang and sings on.

There is a true yearning to respond to
The singing River and the wise Rock.
So say the Asian, the Hispanic, the Jew
The African, the Native American, the Sioux,
The Catholic, the Muslim, the French, the Greek
The Irish, the Rabbi, the Priest, the Sheik,[2]
The Gay, the Straight, the Preacher,
The privileged, the homeless, the Teacher.
They hear. They all hear
The speaking of the Tree.

They hear the first and last of every Tree
Speak to humankind today. Come to me, here
   beside the River.
Plant yourself beside the River.

---

2. Sheik (SHEEK) *n.* an official in the Islamic religion

Each of you, descendant of some passed
On traveller, has been paid for.
You, who gave me my first name, you,
Pawnee, Apache, Seneca, you
Cherokee Nation,[3] who rested with me, then
Forced on bloody feet,
Left me to the employment of
Other seekers—desperate for gain,
Starving for gold.
You, the Turk, the Arab, the Swede, the German, the
   Eskimo, the Scot,

You the Ashanti, the Yoruba, the Kru[4] bought,
Sold, stolen, arriving on the nightmare
Praying for a dream.
Here, root yourselves beside me.
I am that Tree planted by the River,
Which will not be moved.
I, the Rock, I, the River, I, the Tree
I am yours—your passages have been
Lift up your faces, you have a piercing
For this bright morning dawning for you
History, despite its wrenching pain,
Cannot be unlived, but if faced
With courage, need not be lived again.

Lift up your eyes upon
This day breaking for you.
Give birth again
To the dream.

---

3. **Pawnee, Apache, Seneca, Cherokee Nation** (paw-NEE, uh-PACH-ee,
SEHN-ih-kuh, CHER-uh-kee) names of Native American peoples
4. **Ashanti, Yoruba, Kru** (uh-SHAWN-tee, yoh-ROO-buh, KROO) peoples of West Africa

Women, children, men,
Take it into the palms of your hands,
Mold it into the shape of your most
Private need. Sculpt it into
The image of your most public self.
Lift up your hearts
Each new hour holds new chances
For a new beginning.
Do not be wedded forever
To fear, yoked eternally
To brutishness.[5]

The horizon leans forward,
Offering you space to place new steps of change.
Here, on the pulse of this fine day
You may have the courage
To look up and out and upon me, the
Rock, the River, the Tree, your country.
No less to Midas[6] than the mendicant.[7]
No less to you now than the mastodon

Here, on the pulse of this new day
You may have the grace to look up and
And into your sister's eyes, and into
Your brother's face, your country
And say simply
Very simply
With hope—
Good morning.

---

5. brutishness (BROOT-ihsh-nehs) *n.* cruelty
6. Midas (MEYE-duhs) in Greek mythology, a king who was granted
the power of turning everything he touched into gold
7. mendicant (MEHN-dih-kuhnt) *n.* a beggar

AFTER YOU READ

Exchanging Backgrounds and Cultures

1. Do you think Nikki Giovanni and Abiodun Oyewole share similar feelings about being African American? Explain.

2. What important theme about African American life do "Nikki-Rosa" and "Listen Children" share?

3. How does Maya Angelou relate the history of African Americans to that of other peoples in her poem?

What Do You Think?

Which poem in this group is especially meaningful to you? What did you like about the poet's use of language?

Experiencing Poetry

In "Another Mountain," Abiodun Oyewole uses several metaphors to describe his experience of facing and overcoming difficulties in his life. Think of an experience which in some way helped make you stronger. Write a poem about your experience, using metaphors to develop the theme.

Optional Activity Maya Angelou's "On the Pulse of Morning" is a dramatic statement of hope for the future, written for an important occasion. Think of an important event that you participated in or one that you will participate in. Write a poem expressing the importance of the occasion for you.

INTRODUCTION

Section 2:
In Our World

The four poets in this section speak about what makes their world special—Evans and Baraka with passion, and Giovanni and Long with quiet reflection. Mari Evans's poem, "Who Can Be Born Black," is a celebration of African American pride and unity, a typical theme in her work. Born in Toledo, Ohio, in 1923, Evans has been writing since the fourth grade; her poetry appears in many anthologies.

Amiri Baraka's "Ka 'Ba" reflects the poet's commitment to uniting African Americans in an appreciation of their culture. A native of Newark, New Jersey, Baraka emerged in the 1960s as one of the most important African American authors of our time.

Nikki Giovanni has said that she remembers and appreciates the legacies her grandmother and others gave her. "Knoxville, Tennessee" reflects Giovanni's love for the people in her past and the place of her birth.

The poems of Doc (Doughtry) Long appear in many anthologies of African American poetry. In "#4," he looks back, as does Giovanni, to his personal and cultural roots.

#4

by Doughtry Long

Where my grandmother lived
there was always sweet potato pie
and thirds on green beans and
songs and words of how we'd
survived it all.
Blackness.
And the wind
a soft lull
in the pecan tree
whispered
Ethiopia[1]
    Ethiopia, Ethiopia
E-th-io-piaaaaa!

---

1. **Ethiopia** (ee-thee-OH-pee-uh) an ancient kingdom in northeast
   Africa that overlapped what is now modern Ethiopia

Knoxville, Tennessee

by Nikki Giovanni

I always like summer
best
you can eat fresh corn
from daddy's garden
and okra
and greens
and cabbage
and lots of
barbecue
and buttermilk
and homemade ice-cream
at the church picnic
and listen to
gospel music
outside
at the church
homecoming
and go to the mountains with
your grandmother
and go barefooted
and be warm
all the time
not only when you go to bed
and sleep

Ka 'Ba[1]

by Amiri Baraka

A closed window looks down
on a dirty courtyard, and black people
call across or scream across or walk across
defying physics in the stream of their will

Our world is full of sound
Our world is more lovely than anyone's
tho we suffer, and kill each other
and sometimes fail to walk the air

We are beautiful people
with african imaginations
full of masks and dances and swelling chants
with african eyes, and noses, and arms,
though we sprawl in gray chains in a place
full of winters, when what we want is sun.

We have been captured,
brothers. And we labor
to make our getaway, into
the ancient image, into a new

correspondence with ourselves
and our black family. We need magic
now we need the spells, to raise up
return, destroy, and create. What will be

the sacred words?

---

1. *Ka 'Ba* (KAH BAH) a Swahili term that in the Islamic religion
refers to the East-facing position assumed during prayer

Who Can Be Born Black

by Mari Evans

Who
can be born black
and not
sing
the wonder of it
the joy
the challenge

And/to come together
in a coming togetherness
vibrating with the fires of pure knowing
reeling with power
ringing with the sound above sound above sound
to explode/in the majesty of our oneness
our comingtogether
in a comingtogetherness

> Who
> can be born
> black
> and not exult[1]

---

1. **exult** (ehg-ZULT) *v.* to be extremely joyful; rejoice

AFTER YOU READ

Exchanging Backgrounds and Cultures

1. African American unity and pride is at the center of both Evans's and Baraka's poems. How are the poems different?

2. Which two poems celebrate the African heritage of African Americans? Explain.

3. What effect does the poets' choice of images have in both "Knoxville, Tennessee" and "#4"?

What Do You Think?

Which poem do you find most interesting? What did you especially like about it?

Experiencing Poetry

In "Knoxville, Tennessee" and "#4," the poets reflect on positive images from their childhood and the feelings they evoke. Think about people or places from your past that have positive associations for you. Write a poem about your memories, using images to convey your feelings.

Optional Activity In "Ka 'Ba," Baraka celebrates ancient African cultures when he refers to "masks and dances and swelling chants." What would you celebrate from your own cultural heritage? Write a poem reflecting the accomplishments of your ancestors.

UNIT 3: FOCUS ON WRITING

The experience that a poem creates is a result of the poet's careful choice of words, not just for meaning but for sound as well. The special tools of the poet include techniques such as figurative language and repetition.

Writing a Poem

Consider the following topics: someone you admire, a personal triumph, a significant event in your life, an important issue. Write a poem about one of these topics or another topic of your choice.

The Writing Process

Good writing requires both time and effort. An effective writer completes a number of stages that together make up the writing process. The stages of the writing process are given below to help guide you through your assignment.

Prewriting

Once you have chosen a topic, develop a list of images, or word pictures, that relate to your topic. If it is helpful, categorize them according to the senses they involve—sight, taste, hearing, touch, or smell. As you jot down images, aim for fresh comparisons or combinations of words—such as Maya Angelou's "bruising darkness." Such images create strong, lasting impressions on the reader. When you have finished, review your lists and underline the most effective images.

Next, think about what you wish readers of your poem to experience. How do you want them to feel? What do you want them to understand? Once you have determined this, think about how you can accomplish your purpose. Do you want your poem to sound informal like conversation, as in Giovanni's "Nikki-Rosa," or do you want a more formal rhythm? Will you use rhyme? If so, list several words that rhyme with words on your list of images.

Also consider how you want your poem to look. The length of lines and the spaces between words—or even between letters—can be varied to create meaning. In Long's "#4," for instance, the poet has repeated and drawn out the word *Ethiopia,* partly to mimic the sound of the wind in the pecan tree.

Drafting and Revising

Draw from your list of images as you write. After every few lines, pause to read your poem aloud. Do the imagery and the rhythm create the effect you wanted?

When you have finished your first draft, read the entire poem aloud. Revise any lines or words that do not convey the desired sound or meaning.

As with your other writing assignments, you may find it helpful to read it aloud to a friend; give your friend a copy so that he or she can follow as you read. Have your friend identify images or lines that were particularly effective, and the ones that were less so. Talk about the various elements involved—rhyme, rhythm, repetition, imagery, or other poetic devices that you may have used. Revise any parts of the poem that you feel are still weak, and make a final draft.

Proofreading and Publishing

Because contemporary poetry often departs from standard spelling, grammar, punctuation, and capitalization, it is easy to miss a mistake when you proofread. Make sure that any variation is what you intended.

Do you have a place for displaying poetry in your classroom? If so, consider posting your poem. If you have an interest in art, you might illustrate it as well. Ask your teacher, too, about literary magazines or contests that accept submissions from young adults.

UNIT 4

DRAMA OF THE AFRICAN AMERICANS

Since ancient times, audiences have enjoyed the experience provided by drama. Although it shares many features with novels and short stories, drama is special; it is meant to be performed. A play makes characters and situations real in a way that other forms of fiction cannot—you actually see and hear the characters before you. As a member of the audience, you participate by being a witness to the action of the play. Sometimes a playwright even involves the audience directly by having a character address them.

Because a play is meant to be performed rather than read, it must be written in a special format. Most of the written text is **dialogue**—the words that the characters speak. Writing down the words of the characters is not enough, however. The playwright must fill in the details of character, action, and setting with descriptive notes called **stage directions.** Such directions generally are enclosed within parentheses. They may include the smallest gesture by a character as well as a description of an entire stage set for a particular scene.

Whereas a novel is divided into chapters, a play is divided into major sections called **acts.** Within an act, there may be several smaller sections called **scenes.** The excerpt you are about to read is from a one-act play, *Escape to Freedom* by Ossie Davis. Often, actors play more than one role in a drama. You will notice that in his play, Davis has, in fact, created a cast of characters who appear as different people. As you read the play, try to see the stage and hear the voices of the actors.

On the porch of this old house in the South, a *Man with a Trumpet* sits in the hot summer weather. African American artist Gilbert Fletcher is particularly fond of painting Southern scenes such as this one. He has exhibited his work in numerous East Coast museums and galleries, from Harlem to New Orleans. Fletcher's paintings have also been included in several important collections of African American art.

INTRODUCTION
Escape to Freedom

Born in Cogdell, Georgia, in 1917, Ossie Davis began his long career in drama when he joined the Rose McClendon Players in Harlem in 1941. Within a few years, he had played many roles, both on tour and on Broadway. His comedy, *Purlie Victorious,* in which he played the lead role on Broadway, went on to become a successful musical.

In addition to his work in the theater, Davis has directed and produced several films, among them *Cotton Comes to Harlem.* He is probably best known as a television and film actor, however. The roles Davis has played reflect his dedication to increasing public awareness of the plight of African Americans in the United States. As a long-time civil rights activist, Ossie Davis has also participated in marches and testified before Congress.

In the following excerpt from *Escape to Freedom,* Davis provides insight into the nature of prejudice. He uses the story of young Frederick Douglass to speak out against racial prejudice and to show that all people are born free and equal.

from *Escape to Freedom*

by Ossie Davis

THE TIME
The 1830s

THE PLACE
The Eastern Shore of Maryland,
and Baltimore

CAST OF CHARACTERS
Fred Douglass

Black Woman

Black Man

Black Boy

White Woman

White Man

White Boy

Scene One

◆
◆ [*A slave cabin. Behind* FRED, *we see* BLACK WOMAN *enter with candle and kneel beside a dummy baby—young* FRED—*wrapped in a gunny sack and lying on the floor.*]

FRED [*To audience*] My mother's name was Harriet Bailey. I took the name Douglass later in my life. I never saw my mother more than four or five times in my life, and each time was very brief—and always at night.

[BLACK WOMAN *picks up baby and begins singing softly as she rocks it to sleep.* FRED *continues narration under song.*]

BLACK WOMAN

> *Black sheep, black sheep*
>
> *Where'd you lose your lamb?*
>
> *Way down in the valley*
>
> *The birds and the butterflies*
>
> *Are picking out its eyes*

Poor little thing crying mammy

Go and tell Aunt Susie

Go and tell Aunt Susie

Go and tell Aunt Susie

The old gray goose is dead.

FRED She did not live with me, but was hired out by my master to a man who lived about twelve miles down the road, which she had to walk, at night, after she was through working, in order to see me at all. She couldn't stay long, being a field hand—the penalty for not showing up in the fields at sunrise was a severe whipping. It was whispered that my master was my father, but my mother, in the few times I ever got to see her, never told me one way or another.

[BLACK WOMAN *puts baby back on the floor, covers it with a gunny sack, takes one last look, and exits.*]

FRED Long before I waked she would be gone. After my mother died I was sent to live with my Aunt Jenny, but we had almost no time at all to be together. I was one of three or four hundred slaves who lived on the plantation. I was not old enough to work in the fields— I was only about seven at the time. I had no bed, no regular place to sleep, and would probably have died from hunger and cold, except that on the coldest nights I would steal a sack that was used for carrying corn to the mill, and crawl into it, and go to sleep on the cold, damp floor.

[FRED *finds a gunny sack, crawls into it, and tries to cover up for the night, but he is too tall and his feet stick out of the bottom. He tries to find a more comfortable position and finally goes to sleep. A beat, to indicate passage of time. A sudden noise and a light bursting through the door bring*

FRED *awake.* WHITE BOY, *as overseer, bursts in, followed by* BLACK BOY, *as a very frightened young slave.* WHITE BOY, *seeing* FRED *asleep, pushes him with his foot.*]

WHITE BOY Where is she, boy—where is your Aunt Jenny?

FRED [*Scared out of his wits, trying to pull himself together, trying to wake up*] Where is who, sir?

WHITE BOY [*Snatching* FRED *to his feet*] Don't mess with me, boy, you know who I mean! I'm talking about your Aunt Jenny—now, where did she go when she left here last night?

FRED [*Completely in the dark*] My Aunt Jenny wasn't here last night—

[WHITE BOY *turns to* BLACK BOY, *standing nearby, as* WHITE MAN *and* BLACK WOMAN *enter.*]

BLACK BOY That's what she told us when she left the cabin last night, Mr. Gore—said she was coming over here to say good night to Frederick, her nephew—

FRED I ain't seen my Aunt Jenny since a long, long time ago—

WHITE BOY You lie to me, boy, and I'll break your neck.

FRED I ain't lying, Mr. Gore, I ain't lying!

WHITE MAN [*As Colonel Lloyd, to* BLACK BOY] You know what happens to darkies who try to escape from me, don't you?

BLACK BOY Yessir—

WHITE MAN Was your Aunt Jenny in here to see you last night? Tell me the truth—

FRED I am telling the truth, Colonel Lloyd—my Aunt Jenny wasn't here last night.

[WHITE MAN, *satisfied, turns from* FRED. WHITE BOY, *not to be outdone, turns to the other slaves.*]

WHITE BOY Well, if she didn't come here, she must have run away, and if she ran away, she must have had some help–now, who did it? Which one of you lazy, shiftless no-goods helped Jenny escape?

[BLACK WOMAN *and* BLACK BOY, *afraid of what they know is coming, ad-lib*[1] *their earnest denials.*]

BLACK WOMAN *and* BLACK BOY Please, sir, Mr. Gore, we ain't done nothing! It wasn't me, sir! We don't know nothing!

[BLACK MAN *hurries in.*]

BLACK MAN Colonel Lloyd! Colonel Lloyd, sir—

WHITE MAN What is it, Jethro?

BLACK MAN It's Uncle Noah, sir—

WHITE MAN Uncle Noah? What about him?

BLACK MAN Uncle Noah's done escaped, too!

WHITE BOY Oh, my God! They're running off together!

[WHITE BOY *and* WHITE MAN *race off. The three blacks wait until they are sure they are not being observed, then they jump up and down in glee as they celebrate the fact.* FRED *watches, not fully understanding, until he finally manages to get* BLACK MAN's *attention.*]

FRED Uncle Jethro! Uncle Jethro—why you-all dancing?

BLACK MAN [*Trying to keep his voice down*] We celebrating the escape! Jenny and Noah, they done escaped—and

---

1. **ad-lib** (ad-LIHB) *v.* to improvise; make up

we celebrating! If they makes it and don't get caught, it means they *free!* No more having to call some mean old white man your master—

[BLACK MAN *looks around and is suddenly aware that* WHITE MAN *and* WHITE BOY *are at the door and within earshot.* BLACK MAN *grabs* FRED *by the head and pushes him to his knees.* BLACK BOY *and* BLACK WOMAN, *catching on, sink to their knees also.* BLACK MAN *looks upward to heaven as if what follows were a continuation of heartfelt prayer.*]

BLACK MAN Master, master, oh, gracious master, look down from your throne of grace and mercy and catch ol' Noah and Jenny by the scruffs of their no-good necks—

WHITE BOY All right, that's enough of that bull—

BLACK MAN I was just trying to help Colonel Lloyd in this deep, dark hour of his distress—

WHITE BOY Enough, I say—and get out of here, the lot of you, and get into them fields and get to work—now! [*Indicating* FRED] Not you, boy.

[BLACK MAN, BLACK WOMAN, *and* BLACK BOY *hurry out.* WHITE BOY *turns to* WHITE MAN, *indicating* FRED.]

WHITE BOY Colonel, you want me to send this boy to the fields with the rest of them?

WHITE MAN No. All I want from Fred is that he looks after my yard—my flowers, my trees, and my fruit— right, boy?

FRED Yes, sir.

[WHITE MAN *and* WHITE BOY *exit.* FRED *is left alone.* BLACK BOY *and* WHITE WOMAN *enter, as trees in the orchard. They are carrying prop trees, which* FRED *eyes hungrily.*]

FRED [*To audience*] This garden was not the least source of trouble on the plantation. Its excellent fruit was quite a temptation to the hungry swarm of boys, as well as the older slaves. Scarcely a day passed but that some slave had to take the lash for stealing fruit.

[FRED *crosses to one tree and tries to shake loose an apple; no luck. He moves to the other tree and shakes it; an apple falls. He grabs the apple, looks around, and starts offstage as* BLACK MAN *enters and grabs him.*]

BLACK MAN Gotcha!

FRED [*Struggling to free himself*] Let me go—let me go!

BLACK MAN [*Laughing, but still hanging on*] Stealing the Colonel's apples—how about that?

FRED Please, Jethro, let me go!

[BLACK MAN *looks around to see if anyone is looking. Satisfied that the two of them are alone, he lets* FRED *loose.*]

BLACK MAN Colonel catch you stealing his apples, he skin you, boy—

FRED I know, Jethro, but I'm hungry—are you gonna tell?

BLACK MAN There's only one way I know to get you out of this mess, boy, and save your thieving hide.

FRED What's that?

BLACK MAN Consume the evidence, boy—consume the evidence!

[BLACK MAN *takes a huge bite out of the apple and passes the remainder to* FRED.]

FRED Where you been, Jethro?

BLACK MAN [*Grinning as he eats*] Where you think I been, boy?

FRED [*Excited at the prospect*] Baltimore! You been to Baltimore!

BLACK MAN [*Pride of accomplishment*] Right! Boy, you ought to see that place!

[*An angry voice from offstage startles them.*]

BLACK WOMAN [*Offstage*] Fred! Where you at, boy?

[BLACK MAN *pulls* FRED *down and ducks himself just as* BLACK WOMAN *hurries on, carrying a clean shirt.*]

BLACK WOMAN [*Looking around*] Fred—boy, you're gonna get a whipping if you don't watch out!

[BLACK WOMAN *exits. When the coast is clear,* BLACK MAN *and* FRED *raise their heads again.*]

FRED I better git—

[FRED *starts to rise, but* BLACK MAN *pulls him back down.*]

BLACK MAN But I ain't told you what all I seen in Baltimore!

[*Much as* FRED *wants to leave, he cannot give up a chance to hear more.*]

FRED What did you see in Baltimore, Jethro?

BLACK MAN I'll tell you—but only if you promise: every time you shake down some of Colonel Lloyd's apples or oranges or whatnot, you save some for me.

FRED [*Hesitates, then takes the plunge.*] I'll do it, Jethro, I'll do it—now tell me—

BLACK MAN Well, first, there's the streets, wide, long, and all laid out—and on either side, houses to put them to shame.

FRED Do the slaves live in houses?

BLACK MAN Of course they do! They wear shoes—

FRED [*Astounded*] They wear shoes!

BLACK MAN Sometimes—and warm clothes, and sometimes even hats.

FRED Hats? Even when they work in the fields?

BLACK MAN [*Scornful*] Ain't no fields in Baltimore, boy— Baltimore is a city, a great big city. All the slaves there work as house servants, with plenty to eat and drink all the time.

FRED [*Dreaming*] I sure wish I could go to Baltimore!

BLACK MAN [*Expanding*] And that ain't all. Guess what else I seen?

FRED What, Jethro?

BLACK MAN I seen a black man—who was free.

FRED [*Not quite grasping the concept*] Free? You saw a black man who owned himself?

BLACK MAN Yeah—he was a sailor.

[BLACK WOMAN *enters and spots the two.*]

BLACK WOMAN So there you are, both of you—stealing master's fruit!

BLACK MAN Uh. Uh! [BLACK MAN *and* FRED *jump up.*] We ain't stealing. Hard as we work for Colonel Lloyd—and for nothing—we deserve this fruit! It's part of our pay!

BLACK WOMAN Good. I'm sure Colonel Lloyd will be glad to hear that.

BLACK MAN [*Giving up*] Aw, woman—come on, Fred.

[BLACK MAN *and* FRED *start off.*]

BLACK WOMAN No, you don't, Fred Bailey—I got a message from the master.

[BLACK MAN *exits.* FRED *turns to* BLACK WOMAN.]

FRED What message?

BLACK WOMAN First, you're to take off that filthy shirt—
then you're to scrub yourself with soap and water and
get into these clean clothes.

FRED What for?

BLACK WOMAN You're going to Baltimore—

FRED Baltimore!

BLACK WOMAN Master's nephew and his wife need
somebody to help look after the house and their little
boy. Well, don't stand there gawking, boy, get into this
shirt!

[FRED *grins and starts immediately to take off his shirt as
"Bright Glory" song begins offstage.*]

Scene Two

[*While singing "Bright Glory," the cast changes the set to an
arrangement suggesting a neat back yard, with a white picket
fence, a table, and a chair. On the table is a Bible and a plate
of buttered bread.*]

COMPANY

> *You don't hear me praying here*
>
> *You can't find me nowhere (can't find me)*
>
> *Come on up to bright glory*
>
> *I'll be waiting up there*
>
> *I'll be waiting up there, my Lord*

I'll be waiting up there (be waiting)
Come on up to bright glory
I'll be waiting up there.

[COMPANY *continues to hum melody offstage as dialogue continues.*]

[FRED *and* JETHRO *enter.* FRED *is carrying a small bundle. They cross into yard.*]

JETHRO Well, Frederick, here we are.

FRED [*Looking around, taking it all in*] Baltimore.

JETHRO [*Pointing*] And that's the house, right over there. Now, remember, mind your manners; show Mr. and Mrs. Auld what a good little nigger you are—no sass, no back talk, remember your place. Keep your head bowed and your eyes on the ground—and whatever they tell you to do—do it! Right away—understand?

FRED Yes, Jethro, but—do what?

[*Humming offstage ends.*]

JETHRO Don't worry, they'll tell you. Now I got to be going—

FRED But ain't you gonna take me in?

JETHRO Look, Fred, you don't need nobody to take you in. Just obey the white folks—do whatever they tell you, and you'll be all right.

[JETHRO *exits, after a beat.* FRED *turns and takes a few tentative steps toward the house.*]

FRED Here in Baltimore I saw what I had never seen before: it was a white face, beaming with the most kindly emotions—the face of my new mistress, Sophia Auld.

[WHITE WOMAN *enters during above. She sits at the table, picks up the Bible, and begins to read.*]

WHITE BOY [*Enters from house and runs to* WHITE WOMAN.] Mother! Button up my shirt!

WHITE WOMAN I declare, little Thomas, surely the least you can do is button your own shirt.

WHITE BOY I want you to button it!

[WHITE WOMAN *reluctantly puts her Bible aside and buttons his shirt. Then she looks down.*]

WHITE WOMAN And your shoes, Thomas, you haven't even tied your shoes—

WHITE BOY I want you to tie them!

[*Exasperated, she starts to reach down, but catches sight of* FRED, *who has crossed to the back yard and is standing nearby.*]

WHITE WOMAN Fred?

FRED Yes, Miz Sophia.

WHITE WOMAN [*Relieved*] Thank God, you've come at last. Thomas, this is Fred, your slave—your uncle sent him to stay with us and to be your body servant—

WHITE BOY [*Excited by the prospect*] Is he really my slave?

WHITE WOMAN Yes.

WHITE BOY All mine, and nobody else's?

WHITE WOMAN Yes—until your uncle takes him back.

WHITE BOY Good! Come, Fred—

[WHITE BOY *signals* FRED *and starts off.*]

WHITE WOMAN Wait a minute, Thomas, where are you going?

WHITE BOY To the dockyards, to show off my new slave. Come on, Fred—

WHITE WOMAN No, Thomas.

WHITE BOY We'll be right back.

WHITE WOMAN I said no. Your father will be home in a minute, and you haven't read your Bible for today.

WHITE BOY [*Angry*] I don't want to read the Bible for today. I want to show off my slave—

WHITE WOMAN [*Firmly*] There'll be plenty of time for that later. Now we read from the Bible.

[WHITE WOMAN *picks up the Bible, finds the place, and hands it to* WHITE BOY.]

WHITE BOY [*Takes the book and pretends to try, then gives up.*] I don't want to—

WHITE WOMAN Come on, Thomas, show Freddie how well you can read.

WHITE BOY [*Shouting*] I don't want to!

[*He flings the book down and runs into the house.*]

WHITE WOMAN Thomas! Thomas, honey, Mother didn't mean to hurt your feelings—

[*She hurries off after him.* FRED *stands a minute; then, his curiosity getting the better of him, he picks up the Bible, opens it, trying to understand what is meant by reading.* WHITE WOMAN *re-enters, carrying a pair of sandals.* FRED *is so occupied he does not see her. She approaches and looks over his shoulder.*]

WHITE WOMAN Fred—

FRED [*Startled, putting the book down like a hot potato*] Yes, ma'am—[*He stands before her, guilty, his head bowed, his eyes cast down in a manner he has been taught is proper for a slave.*]

WHITE WOMAN [*Chiding, but kindly*] No, no, Fred, you mustn't bow your head to me like that. We are all of us still God's children—nor slave nor master makes a difference to Him. It says so in the Bible—this book right here that you had in your hand.

[FRED, *remembering his guilt, casts his eyes down again.*]

FRED I'm sorry, ma'am, I didn't mean to touch it, but—

WHITE WOMAN Fred—

FRED [*Still not looking up*] Yes, ma'am—

WHITE WOMAN Here are some sandals for you to wear.

[FRED *cannot manage to speak.*]

Take them.

[*He takes them.*]

Put them on, they're yours.

[FRED *tries to put the sandals on but is too nervous.*]

Would you like for me to help you?

[*She kneels and puts the sandals on* FRED, *who is stunned at such kind and gentle behavior from a white person.*]

There you are—

[FRED *stands before her, dumb, his eyes cast down, unable to say a word.*]

[*Kindly, with complete understanding*] Don't you know how to say thank you?

FRED [*Not daring to look up at her, he finally manages it.*] Thank you, ma'am.

WHITE WOMAN [*Suddenly occurring to her*] My lands, child, you must be starved. Have some bread and butter.

[*She turns to the table and offers it to him.* FRED *takes it but can't seem to manage to get it into his mouth.*]

WHITE WOMAN Is something the matter?

FRED [*Quickly*] No, ma'am—it's just that—

WHITE WOMAN Yes?

[FRED *looks intently at the Bible. It is not difficult for her to read his thoughts.*]

Would you like for me to teach you to read?

FRED Oh, yes, ma'am!

[*She picks up the Bible and hands it to him.* FRED *quickly puts his bread aside and picks up the Bible, getting great pleasure out of just being able to hold a book in his hands.*]

WHITE WOMAN This is the Bible, and it is spelled B-I-B-L-E.

[FRED *looks at her in total confusion.*]

What I mean is: "Bible" is a word—

[*She stops and studies him. It is obvious that he has absolutely no understanding of anything she is telling him. She sits and pulls him to her, takes the book into her own hands, and begins pointing out each letter.*]

—and every word is made up of letters, which we call the alphabet.

FRED Alphabet.

WHITE WOMAN Good. Now, the letter of the alphabet we use to begin the word "Bible" is called "B"—

FRED "B"—

WHITE WOMAN Very good, Fred, excellent. And this letter of the alphabet is called "I."

FRED "I"—

[WHITE MAN, *as Hugh Auld, enters and stops, scarcely believing his eyes.*]

WHITE WOMAN Now the third letter in the word "Bible" is the same as the first letter of the word—

FRED [*Snapping it up*] "B"!

WHITE WOMAN [*Overjoyed at his obvious intelligence*] Excellent, Fred, excellent!

WHITE MAN [*Shouting*] Sophia, stop!

[*He dashes over and snatches the Bible from his wife's hand.*] What are you doing?

WHITE WOMAN I'm teaching Freddie to read—

WHITE MAN Freddie?

WHITE WOMAN You asked your uncle to send you a slave to be a companion to little Thomas. Freddie, this is Mr. Hugh Auld, your new master while you are in Baltimore.

[FRED *tries to find a proper response, but just at this moment* WHITE BOY *runs back on and grabs* FRED *by the arm and starts to pull.*]

WHITE BOY Come on, Fred, I've got something to show you.

[FRED *looks to* WHITE WOMAN—*and* WHITE MAN—*for instructions.*]

Fred—I'm not ever gonna let you be my slave if you don't come on; I want to show you my new boat. Tell him, Mama—

WHITE WOMAN [*Smiling*] It's all right, Fred.

[*A beat, then* FRED *and* WHITE BOY, *smiling at each other, run off.* WHITE MAN *watches them off, and then, to make sure he will not be overheard, he takes* WHITE WOMAN *by the arm and draws her aside.*]

WHITE MAN What on earth are you trying to do to that boy, ruin him?

WHITE WOMAN Ruin him? I was only teaching him to read.

WHITE MAN But you can't do that, Sophia!

WHITE WOMAN Why not? He's a very bright boy.

WHITE MAN He's a slave—and to teach a slave to read is not only unlawful, it's unsafe, and I forbid it.

[FRED *starts back onstage in search of the bundle he was carrying, which he has left behind, but, hearing himself being talked about, he starts back out, then stops in a spot where he will not be seen, and listens.*]

WHITE WOMAN [*Deeply disturbed*] Forbid it? But Freddie is human, and the Bible says—

WHITE MAN Never mind what the Bible says—and for Heaven's sakes, stop talking like an abolitionist![2]

WHITE WOMAN Abolitionist?

WHITE MAN Yes, those Yankee do-gooders, always trying to tell us Southerners that black folks are no different from the rest of us—can you imagine such nonsense? Freddie is not human, not in the ways that you and I are.

---

2. **abolitionist** (ab-uh-LIHSH-uh-nihst) *n.* one who wants to do away with slavery

WHITE WOMAN How can you say that of a creature that has a soul and a mind?

WHITE MAN But, darling, Freddie hasn't got a soul—he's black; he's a slave.

WHITE WOMAN But all the same—

WHITE MAN Listen to me, Sophia—reading's not only no good for a black boy like Fred; it would do him harm, make him discontent, miserable, unhappy with his lot. Now, you wouldn't want that, would you?

[WHITE WOMAN *ponders a moment.*]

WHITE WOMAN No, but—

WHITE MAN [*As they exit*] The worst thing in the world you can do for a slave—if you want to keep him happy—is to teach that slave to read, understand?

[*From offstage we hear a low humming, which continues under the following.*]

[*When* WHITE MAN *and* WHITE WOMAN *have gone,* FRED *comes out of hiding.*]

FRED [*To audience*] My master's words sank deep into my heart. I now understood something that had been the greatest puzzle of all to me: the white man's power to enslave the black man. Keep the black man away from the books, keep us ignorant, and we would always be his slaves! From that moment on I understood the pathway from slavery to freedom. Come hell or high water—even if it cost me my life—I was determined to read!

[*Humming ends.*]

[FRED *looks around to make sure he is not being watched, then crosses to pick up the Bible, and tries to read. He walks up and down mumbling to himself, trying to make sense out of the words on the page, but without success. So deep in his preoccupation is he that he does not see that WHITE WOMAN has returned and stands for a moment watching. Not until he bumps into her does he lift his eyes.*]

FRED [*Apologetic, frightened*] Oh—Miz Sophia!

WHITE WOMAN Fred, I made a mistake—about trying to teach you to read—it's—it's not right—it's against the law.

FRED Why is it against the law?

WHITE WOMAN [*Snapping, trying to steel herself for what she has to do*] Don't ask me why, it just is, that's all. And if I catch you with a book, I'll have to take it away, understand?

FRED No, ma'am.

WHITE WOMAN You *do* understand. You are not dumb— you have a good brain in that head of yours.

FRED But if I do have a brain, then how—

WHITE WOMAN And, anyway, you're my property. I own you like I own a horse or a mule. You don't *need* to read, you understand?

FRED [*Tentative, searching, earnest, really trying*] You said that all people was equal before God—that being slave or being free didn't matter before God—

WHITE WOMAN I am not talking about God! And anyway, what God said—about people being equal— doesn't apply to you.

FRED Why don't it, Miz Sophia?

WHITE WOMAN [*Growing more testy*] Because you ain't people, that's why—

FRED But, ma'am, if I ain't people—what am I?

WHITE WOMAN You are—some kind of animal that— that looks like people but you're not!

FRED But I can talk—and you just said I got a good brain—

WHITE WOMAN Don't you contradict me!

FRED And I could read, too, if—

WHITE WOMAN [*Shouting*] You will not read! Not in my house you won't! And if I should ever catch you—

FRED But, please, Miz Sophia—

WHITE WOMAN Shut your sassy, impudent mouth and get out of here! Get out of here!

[WHITE WOMAN *is disturbed by what she has just done. Clutching the Bible, she hurries off.*]

[*Humming begins offstage.*]

FRED [*To audience*] Master Hugh wasted no time. With Miz Sophia's sudden change, I began to see that slavery was harmful to the slaveowner as well as the slave. As the months passed, if I was in a separate room for any length of time, she would search me out, sure that I had found a book—but by now it was too late. The first step had already been taken: Mistress Sophia, by teaching me what little she had, had set my feet on the highway to freedom, and I wasn't going to let her—or anybody else—turn me around.

[*Humming ends.*]

[WHITE BOY *enters, this time as a schoolboy. He is barefoot, his clothes are patched and ragged; he is obviously much worse off than* FRED. FRED *watches as* WHITE BOY *passes, drawn like a magnet by the schoolbooks he carries under his arms.* FRED *suddenly has an idea, and as* WHITE BOY *passes, he snatches up the remainder of the bread and butter on the table and runs after him.*]

FRED Hey! Hey, boy!

[WHITE BOY *does not notice him.*]

Hey, boy, wait—

[*Still no reaction*]

Hey, white boy!

WHITE BOY You calling me?

FRED Yeah, I'm calling you—what's your name?

WHITE BOY My name's Robert. What's yours?

FRED My name's Fred. I'm a slave.

WHITE BOY I know that—well, I gotta go.

[*He starts off, but* FRED *overtakes him.*]

FRED Hey, does your father own slaves?

WHITE BOY No—

FRED Why not?

WHITE BOY [*Embarrassed*] We're too poor. We don't even have enough to eat.

[FRED *looks at* WHITE BOY. WHITE BOY *starts off again.* FRED *conspicuously*[3] *brings the bread into view.*]

FRED Hey, you hungry?

[WHITE BOY *stops, thinks a moment, then turns just in time to see* FRED *shove a big chunk of bread into his mouth.* WHITE BOY *says nothing.* FRED, *seeing the fish is hooked, chews lustily.*]

FRED Man, this is the best bread I ever tasted.

[FRED *breaks off a piece and holds it out.*]

Want a piece?

---

3. *conspicuously* (kun-SPIHK-yoo-uhs-lee) *adv.* in a way that is easily seen or obvious

[WHITE BOY *hesitates a moment, then crosses over to* FRED. *He reaches for the bread, but* FRED *pulls it back.*]

First, you got to answer me a question—you go to school?

WHITE BOY [*Eyes fastened hypnotically on the bread*] Yes.

FRED That means you know how to read, right?

WHITE BOY Yes—

FRED Good.

[FRED *hands* WHITE BOY *the remainder of the bread.* WHITE BOY *puts his books down, the better to deal with the bread, which he snatches and wolfs down hungrily.* FRED, *with equal hunger, snatches up the book and tries to read. When* WHITE BOY *is finished, he wipes his mouth and reaches for his book.*]

WHITE BOY Can I have my book now?

FRED Sure, as soon as you teach me how to read.

WHITE BOY It's against the law to teach you to read. You are a slave.

FRED Are you a slave?

WHITE BOY Of course I'm not a slave—I'm white—

FRED You are white, and you will be free all your life—but I am black—

WHITE BOY [*Thinking about it*]—which means that you will be a slave all your life.

FRED [*Vehemently*] I don't think that's right, do you?

WHITE BOY [*Pondering for a moment*] No!

FRED Then teach me to read—

WHITE BOY What?

FRED Master Auld say, teach a slave to read and he won't be a slave no more.

WHITE BOY He did?

FRED Yes—so as soon as I learn to read I'll be free, just like you. Teach me, Robert—teach me to read from your book—will you?

[WHITE BOY *begins to respond to* FRED*'s enthusiasm.*]

WHITE BOY [*Excited*] Of course I will.

[*They take the book between them as they sit down on the floor—then they begin.*]

WHITE BOY First, the alphabet—"A"—

FRED "A"—

WHITE BOY "B"—

FRED "B"—

WHITE BOY "C"—

FRED "C"—

WHITE BOY "D"—

FRED "D"—

[*So caught up are they in the lesson that they do not see that* WHITE WOMAN *has entered and is spying on them.*]

WHITE BOY "E"—

FRED "E"—

WHITE BOY "F"—

FRED "F"—

[WHITE WOMAN *sneaks up behind the two boys on the floor.*]

WHITE BOY "G"—

FRED "G"—

WHITE BOY "H"—

[WHITE WOMAN *snatches the book from* WHITE BOY's *fingers.* FRED *and* WHITE BOY *jump up.*]

WHITE WOMAN Caught you!

[*She tears the book up and flings the pieces to the ground.*]

WHITE BOY Please, ma'am, we was only—

WHITE WOMAN I know what you were doing—ruining a perfectly good slave! Now get out of here!

[*She hands broom to* FRED.]

And you get to your work!

[*She chases* WHITE BOY *offstage.*]

FRED [*Crosses to pick up the torn pages of the book.*] From this time on she watched me like a hawk—because everything I could find with print on it I tried to read, even if I couldn't understand it all the time.

[FRED *opens the book and begins to read.*]

[*Offstage we hear voices singing "Lord I Don't Feel No Ways Tired."*]

COMPANY

> *I am seeking for a city*
> *Hallelujah*
> *I am seeking for a city*
> *Hallelujah*
> *For a city into the heaven*
> *Hallelujah*
> *For a city into the heaven*
> *Hallelujah*

CHILDREN

    Lord I don't (I don't) feel no ways tired

COMPANY

    Oh glory hallelujah

    For I hope to shout glory when this world is on fire

CHILDREN

    Oh glory hallelujah

[*During the song* FRED, *subconsciously responding to the beat of the music, moves across the stage, reading with one eye and keeping watch with the other. He exits and immediately re-enters, this time carrying a newspaper.*]

[*The cast continues humming the melody of the song from offstage as* FRED *continues.*]

FRED [*Reading aloud*] The general sentiment of mankind is that a man who will not fight for himself, when he has the means to do so, is not worth—

[*He throws newspaper to the ground in frustration.*]

FRED [*To audience*] As I read, I began to realize how much had been denied me as a slave. But my reading didn't show me the way to escape. I finally felt that learning to read had been not a blessing but a curse. Like Master said—the more I read, the more miserable I became.

[WHITE BOY *and* WHITE WOMAN *enter, laughing, hugging, and kissing each other. He is dressed as a sailor and she as a . . . gaudy⁴ woman of the town. They continue . . . laughing; neither is aware that* FRED, *made somewhat bold by his anger, is watching them.*]

---

4. gaudy (GAW-dee) *adj.* bright and showy, but lacking in good taste

WHITE WOMAN [*Finally pulling free*] I've got to go now.

WHITE BOY I'll go with you.

WHITE WOMAN No, you wait here, till I come back.

[*She starts off, but* WHITE BOY *pulls her back.*]

WHITE BOY How about a little something to last me till you return?

[*She laughs as he pulls her to him.*]

WHITE WOMAN You Yankee sailors are all devils, aren't you?

WHITE BOY Sure are!

[*He grabs her, spins her around, and they kiss. Suddenly she spots* FRED *and pulls free again.*]

WHITE WOMAN What are you looking at, boy?

[FRED *is still a slave, but manages, out of his anger, to stand his ground.*]

I'm talking to you, nigger!

WHITE BOY Aw, let the fellow alone.

WHITE WOMAN He's a slave.

WHITE BOY So what—he's still human.

WHITE WOMAN He's a slave, and he's got no business spying on people in a public place. He ought to be whipped!

WHITE BOY Aw, honey, you can't mean that—he's only a kid!

WHITE WOMAN I do mean it. I don't know how you all treat 'em up North, but down here in Maryland—

WHITE BOY All right, all right, you run right along and I'll take care of it.

WHITE WOMAN Ought to be whipped, that's what!

WHITE BOY I'll take care of it—you run on along—

[*She starts offstage.*]

—and hurry back!

[WHITE WOMAN *exits. The sailor, obviously a good-natured man, chuckles as he crosses to* FRED, *who, though frightened, is determined, for the first time, to stand his ground.*]

WHITE BOY You're the first person I ever met who was a slave.

FRED Yeah, but that don't make me no different from you or her or anybody else.

WHITE BOY [*Laughing*] I didn't say it did.

FRED I got brains just like you got brains, and I can think just as good as you can think, and I can read just as good as you can read!

WHITE BOY [*Trying to explain it, but not knowing how*] Look, son, I know how you feel.

FRED How can you know how I feel? You're not black.

WHITE BOY No, I'm not black, and I'm not a slave—but if I were, I'd do something about it.

FRED [*His curiosity overcoming his feelings*] Do what?

WHITE BOY I'd run away first chance I got.

FRED [*Suspicious*] Why should I run away?

WHITE BOY [*Matter-of-factly*] Why stay?

[FRED, *not sure that this is not a trap, refuses to answer directly.*]

FRED I knew a slave who ran away once—but they caught him and beat him and sold him down the river.

WHITE BOY They might catch you—that's a chance you'll have to take—but if you don't take the chance, you'll never be free, right?

FRED But where could I go?

WHITE BOY You could go up north—there are people up north doing all they can to end slavery.

FRED What people?

WHITE BOY Abolitionists—white people and black people, who hate slavery as much as you do. They'd hide you, feed you, give you clothes and money. As a matter of fact, I heard about a young fellow who dressed himself in a sailor suit, like mine, and wrote himself a pass.

FRED A pass? What's that?

WHITE BOY A pass is a little slip of paper a master gives to a slave when he sends him on an errand by himself.

FRED This slave you're talking about—he wrote out his own pass, you say?

WHITE BOY Yes, he signed his master's name to it and then went down to the boat, and got right on, big as you please. Anybody asked him what he was doing, he'd show them his pass, written in his own hand, and tell them he was traveling on business for his master.

FRED And he got away?

WHITE BOY All the way to New York. And if he did it, so can you. Look—as a matter of fact—

[*He reaches into his pocket and brings out a piece of paper and a pencil.*]—I'll show you how. Here, take this and write down what I tell you.

[FRED *seats himself on a convenient object, takes the paper and pencil, and holds them in readiness.*]

"This pass will certify that—"

[FRED *starts to write but stops.*]

What's the matter?

FRED [*Just discovering this fact himself*] I can't write.

WHITE BOY Can't write? But I thought you said—

FRED I said I could read—I taught myself how to read—but not to write.

WHITE BOY Oh, I see.

[*Pauses a moment, then makes a decision.*]

All right, I'll teach you to write.

[*He takes pencil and paper from* FRED *and proceeds to demonstrate. Writing*] This—pass—will—certify—that—[*To* FRED] What did you say your name was?

FRED My name is Frederick.

[*Looks up and sees* WHITE WOMAN, *who has returned and is watching.*

WHITE WOMAN [*Suspicious—to sailor*] What are you doing?

WHITE BOY I was just teaching young Frederick to—

FRED [*Rising in agitation*] No, he wasn't! He wasn't doing no such thing!

WHITE WOMAN Down here it's against the law to teach slaves to read and write.

WHITE BOY [*Laughing*] Who's teaching anybody anything?

[*He rises, looking at her.*]

My, but don't you look wonderful!

[*He holds the paper and pencil behind his back and gestures for* FRED *to take them from him.*]

WHITE WOMAN [*Eating it up*] I do? I went all the way back home just to get these earrings; I do hope you like them—

WHITE BOY Like them? Hon, I love them!

[*Takes her by the arm and starts off.*]

Just wait till I get you downtown so the rest of the boys can see you!

[*He manages to get the pencil and paper back to* FRED *without her noticing, and then they exit.* FRED *watches after them a moment, then turns in high excitement to resume his story.*]

FRED [*To audience*] There was no better place in all Baltimore to start the second part of my education than right where I was—in the shipyard.

[*We hear the cast humming "Lord I Don't Feel No Ways Tired" as they change the set to an arrangement suggesting a shipyard, with coils of rope, planks, etc., strewn about the stage. This continues under the following.*]

I remember seeing ship's carpenters at the dock cut pieces of timber into planks—

[FRED *crosses to a plank, picks it up and examines it.*]

They would write on the plank with a piece of chalk the part of the ship for which it was intended.

[FRED *holds the plank in such a way that he can clearly see the letter "L" that has been handwritten upon it.*]

"L," that's for larboard.

[FRED *takes a piece of chalk and laboriously writes several imitations of the "L," using an appropriate spot on the pier, or on the board, as a blackboard. When he is satisfied, he sets the plank down and picks up another.*]

"S," for starboard.

[FRED *repeats the previous action during the following, putting one plank down as soon as he is finished, and picking up another.*]

"L.F.," that's for larboard forward; "S.A.," that's for starboard aft. In a short while I could do "L," "S," "F," and "A" with no trouble at all.

[*He indicates his mastery with a flourish.*]

And not only planks—during this time any board wall or brick fence or pavement that had any writing on it became my copybook.

[FRED *moves quickly from one appropriate place, construction, or object to another, copying the indicated lettering. In his movings about, he finds a half-torn book.*]

I found a Webster Spelling Book that had written script in it.

[FRED *busily copies from the book, making the lettering on every nearby object.* WHITE BOY *and* WHITE WOMAN, *as children, enter, skipping, and hand their copybooks to* FRED.]

When my little white friends finished with their lettering books at school, they gave them to me.

[FRED *takes the books, thanks* WHITE BOY *and* WHITE WOMAN, *who exit, and then* FRED *goes busily to work.*]

I copied—and copied—and copied—until I had mastered every letter of the alphabet. "Z"!

[FRED *writes a final "Z" on some appropriate surface, then stands back, in pride and satisfaction, to admire his handiwork: every place he looks, everything he sees, has some evidence of FRED's capacity to write.*]

I was now ready to try my hand at the most important thing of all: writing a pass.

COMPANY [*Offstage*]
Lord I don't (I don't) feel no ways tired

CHILDREN
Oh glory hallelujah

COMPANY
For I hope to shout glory when this world is on fire

CHILDREN
Oh glory hallelujah

FRED [*Takes out pencil and paper, reading as he writes.*] This—is—to—certify—that I—the undersigned—have given the bearer, my servant, Fred Bailey, full liberty to go to—

[FRED *looks up and sees* BLACK MAN, *as* JETHRO, *standing over him.*]

Hey, Jethro, look what I just did—

[*Something about* JETHRO*'s face makes him stop.*]

JETHRO [*Sadly*] Ol' Master's dead, Fred.

FRED Dead? Colonel Lloyd?

JETHRO Yes, so all the slaves is being called back to the plantation so the property can be divided up.

FRED Jethro, I can't go back—with this pass I can get to—

JETHRO What?

FRED Never mind.

JETHRO I was sent to get you, and if you don't come, I'm in trouble, and you, too. Come on, Fred.

[JETHRO *exits.* FRED *starts to exit with him, but turns back to the audience.*]

Scene Three

[*During the following, the cast moves the set to an arrangement suggesting a rough country farm.* FRED'*s demeanor*[5] *is different—it is obvious that he is now involved in hard work for the first time in his entire life—work for which he is entirely unsuited.*]

FRED [*To audience*] The whole dream of my life had been to escape from slavery. Yet here I was at seventeen years of age, still a slave, back at St. Michael's on a farm, being forced to do things I had never done before: what good would my reading and writing do me now? In Baltimore with Master Hugh I had at least been fed well enough and given shoes and decent clothes—and there was always the chance that somehow I might escape! But not here at St. Michael's—Master Thomas and his wife, Rowena, not only watched me like a hawk, night and day, but also they were the meanest and stingiest people I ever saw in my life.

[WHITE MAN *enters, as Thomas Auld, dressed for church, moving across the stage. He speaks as he moves.*]

WHITE MAN Don't just stand there gawking, boy, go hitch the horse and buggy.

FRED Yes, sir, but first could we maybe have a little breakfast?

---

5. *demeanor* (dih-MEEN-uhr) *n.* outward behavior

WHITE MAN [*Stops and turns to* FRED] So, looks like you've been in Baltimore too long, boy—my brother, Hugh, and that fancy wife of his have near-about ruined you, I suspect—just look at him, all fat and sassy—dressed up good as any white man—I bet you think you are as good as a white man, don't you, boy? And drop your eyes when I'm talking to you!

[FRED *does so.*]

That's better.

[WHITE MAN *turns and exits.*]

FRED [*To audience*] And his wife, Rowena—

[WHITE WOMAN, *as Rowena Auld, enters, also dressed for church, and moves rapidly across in opposite direction.*]

WHITE WOMAN This ain't Balitmore, boy—you heard Mr. Thomas—get the horse and buggy. We're late already!

FRED [*Tries to stop her*] Yes, ma'am, but we ain't had nothing to eat!

[*She exits.* FRED *shouts after her.*]

You expect us black folks to work around this damned old farm like dogs and you won't even feed us!

[*He turns to face the audience again, and as he speaks the stage is being changed to suggest the interior of a church.*]

It was bad: if we slaves hadn't learned to *steal* in order to feed and to clothe ourselves, we might have died from hunger and exposure.

[*The* COMPANY *has assembled on stage as if they were in church.* WHITE BOY, *dressed as a minister, Cookman, holds a Bible in his hand.* WHITE MAN *and* WHITE WOMAN *are his white audience, standing in the front row. Behind them are the slaves:* BLACK MAN, BLACK WOMAN, *and* BLACK BOY, *who are looking on with interest. They are humming "Give Me That Old-Time Religion."*]

FRED But one night my master and his wife went to a revival meeting. And something totally unexpected happened.

[FRED *moves to join the slaves in the back row as the song begins.*]

COMPANY

> *Give me that old-time religion*
> *Give me that old-time religion*
> *Give me that old-time religion*
> *It's good enough for me*

> *Give me that old-time religion*
> *Give me that old-time religion*
> *Give me that old-time religion*
> *It's good enough for me*

BLACK WOMAN

> *It was good for my old mother*
> *It was good for my old mother*
> *It was good for my old mother*
> *It's good enough for me*

COMPANY

> *Give me that old-time religion*
> *Give me that old-time religion*
> *Give me that old-time religion*
> *It's good enough for me*

BLACK WOMAN

> *It was good enough for master*
> *It was good enough for master*
> *It was good enough for master*
> *It's good enough for me*

[*During the song* WHITE MAN *has been trembling; now he jumps as if suddenly struck by lightning. He dances, shouts, groans, and falls writhing to the floor in the complete ecstasy of religious conversion.*]

WHITE MAN Oh Lord, I'm saved!

WHITE BOY Hallelujah!

WHITE MAN I've been redeemed!

WHITE BOY Oh, glory!

WHITE MAN I love everybody!

[WHITE BOY *and the rest respond with fervor:* "Amen!" "Hallelujah!" Oh, give praises!"]

Everybody is my brother!

[WHITE MAN *runs around the stage in his frenzy, grabbing, hugging, shaking hands with black and white. Even* FRED *responds to this, his hope being—as is that of all the slaves—that the master's conversion will make life better.*]

Everybody is my sister! I love everybody! There is peace in my heart! There is joy in my soul! I love everybody! I love everybody!

[WHITE WOMAN *and* WHITE BOY *help* WHITE MAN *offstage.* FRED *follows them with his eyes, then turns again to the audience, while the* COMPANY *rearranges the set to suggest a Sunday-school classroom.*]

FRED Could it be true? Could it be that my master had really changed? Had he really come to believe that everybody—including black slaves like me—were really his brothers and sisters?

[*To* WHITE BOY, *who has entered with an armload of books and papers*] Do you believe it, Mr. Cookman? Do you believe Master Thomas has really changed?

WHITE BOY God moves in mysterious ways—his wonders to perform. Here, help me with these.

[FRED *takes some of the books and papers from his arms and helps distribute them to the slaves, who are sitting on the benches waiting for the lesson to begin.*]

FRED You really think Master Thomas is going to allow us to hold Sunday school for the rest of the slaves?

WHITE BOY Frederick—where is your faith?

FRED [*To audience*] Mr. Cookman was a fine man, a member of our church who hated slavery as much as I did, and he and I had decided to set up a Sunday school in a house nearby.

[FRED *crosses in to scene.*]

WHITE BOY [*To the class*] Though you are slaves and I am not, in God's sight all men are equal, all men are brothers.

[BLACK WOMAN *stands to ask a question.*]

BLACK WOMAN Is Master Thomas equal too?

WHITE BOY Master Thomas is a Christian; he has accepted Christ, and that means—

[BLACK MAN *rises.*]

BLACK MAN That means all mens, and all womens, are Master Thomas's brothers and sisters—no matter they black or white—ain't that right, Fred?

FRED [*Skeptical*] We'll see. We'll see. Now, the purpose of this Sunday school is to teach you—all of you—to read and write.

[BLACK WOMAN *rises.*]

BLACK WOMAN Do reading and writing make people free?

[FRED *and* WHITE BOY *look at each other.*]

WHITE BOY No, I'm afraid not, but—

FRED —but it can help. For instance, there was a slave in Baltimore who learned to read and write, and the first thing he did was to write himself a pass—

BLACK WOMAN A pass?

FRED A pass is a piece of paper, like this—

[*Shows slave's pass.*]

—with writing on it—like this—that says: this black man, or this black woman, is free.

[*He looks at each of them intently.*]

BLACK MAN You mean—if I had a paper like that—I'd be free?

FRED Well, down here in Maryland where everybody know that you and me belong to Master Thomas, no. But if you were to run away and go up north to Pennsylvania or to New York—

BLACK WOMAN You can read, Fred, and you can write?

FRED Yes, I can.

BLACK WOMAN Well, in that case, why ain't *you* run away? Why ain't *you* free?

[FRED *and* WHITE BOY *look at each other.*] . . .

[WHITE MAN, *carrying a whip, and* WHITE WOMAN, *brandishing a broom, come running in, shouting.*]

WHITE MAN *and* WHITE WOMAN Caught you, caught you, caught you!

[WHITE MAN *starts beating the slaves with his whip.* WHITE WOMAN *takes after* FRED *with her broom.*]

WHITE MAN Teach slaves to read and write, will you? Over my dead body!

[FRED *and the other slaves are driven off.* WHITE MAN *picks up a fallen book and waves it in the face of* WHITE BOY.*]

WHITE BOY But you're converted, Master Thomas, you're a Christian!

WHITE MAN Get off my property! Before I take my gun and blow you off! And take your filthy junk with you!

[WHITE BOY *quickly gathers up whatever books and papers have fallen, and exits.*]

Dirty abolitionist—

WHITE WOMAN You *know* who's behind all this, don't you? You know who started it?

WHITE MAN Frederick?

WHITE WOMAN Frederick! Reading, writing, all them books—I warned you.

WHITE MAN But I took his books. I threw them away.

WHITE WOMAN Don't do no good, taking 'em—he always seems to find some more somewhere—

WHITE MAN And now he's teaching the *others* to read and write—that's what makes him so dangerous. What are we to do with that boy, Rowena?

[*They both ponder a moment; then* WHITE WOMAN *has an idea.*]

WHITE WOMAN Well, there is one thing we can do: we can send him to Covey's.

WHITE MAN Send him to Covey's—why didn't I think of that?

WHITE WOMAN Covey will break him—

WHITE MAN Of course—we'll send that arrogant, bullheaded boy to Covey's!

[*They exit smiling.*] . . .

AFTER YOU READ

Exchanging Backgrounds and Cultures

1. How does this play show that the arguments used to justify slavery were weak?

2. What basic human rights do we take for granted today that were denied to young Frederick and other slaves?

3. What did Frederick see as the key to his freedom? Why?

What Do You Think?

How did you feel about the main character in this play? What overall effect do you think the playwright intended?

Experiencing Drama

Anyone who tried teaching young Frederick to read was taking a personal risk because it was against the law to do so. Think about other places and times in which people have taken personal risks to help others. Write a scene based on such a situation. Make sure that you provide your audience with enough background through dialogue or stage directions.

Optional Activity In this play, young Frederick Douglass realizes that he must rely on himself if he is to be free. Think about a time when you had to draw on your own inner strength in order to overcome a problem or obstacle. Did the situation involve a conflict with anyone else? How did you deal with it? Write a scene from a play in which the main character faces such a problem. Include whatever stage directions you feel are necessary for developing setting, character, and background.

UNIT 4: FOCUS ON WRITING

When writing a play, a playwright has the challenging task of developing plot, character, and theme through the dialogue—the characters' words. Important details must be put in stage directions so that directors, set designers, and actors correctly interpret the characters, action, and setting. The play then comes to life when it is performed on stage.

Writing a Dramatic Scene

A scene has the same form as a full-length play, with a beginning, a middle, and an end. Write a dramatic scene about a family gathering, a historical event, or a topic of your choice.

The Writing Process

Good writing requires both time and effort. An effective writer completes a number of stages that together make up the writing process. The stages of the writing process are given below to help guide you through your assignment.

Prewriting

Brainstorm ideas that you might want to write about. Do you keep a journal? You might find several ideas in it. Then organize your ideas in a list. Once you have chosen your topic, consider the theme you want to develop and the effect you want your play to have on an audience.

Before you write, prepare a list of characters and briefly identify each one. Save details of dress or physical appearance for stage directions in the play itself.

Next, make notes about the setting of your scene—the time of year and the place. Remember that when choosing setting and events, you must be able to present them in the limited space of a stage. Often you can suggest the setting with a few props, or movable objects. In the second scene of *Escape to Freedom,* for instance, a neat Baltimore yard is suggested by a white picket fence. Include in your notes a list of the props and the costumes you might need.

At this point, you can outline the plot. Where does the scene begin? Who is the main character? What problem does he or she face? Is the conflict resolved in this scene? How does the scene end?

Drafting and Revising

Refer to your lists and plot outline as you write the first draft of your scene. Remember that you will revise later.

After preparing your list of characters, write stage directions that set the scene. Your directions should allow a reader to imagine the setting easily and should tell a director and actors exactly how you want your scene to look.

Use the play format to begin writing the dialogue. Place a character's name at the left of your page, followed by a colon, and then write the character's words. You can include additional stage directions about action or tone of voice in parentheses within parts of the dialogue.

Once you finish your first draft, read it aloud to a partner so you can hear how the words will sound on a stage. Does the dialogue sound like natural conversation? Revise any parts that you feel do not sound natural or do not convey what you intended. Eliminate anything that is unrelated to the scene.

Proofreading and Publishing

Proofread your scene, correcting any errors in spelling, grammar, punctuation, and capitalization. Then prepare a neat final copy.

Now you are ready to publish your work. Have willing friends or classmates perform the scene for the rest of the class or for other classes in your school.

LITERATURE ACKNOWLEDGMENTS

ABIODUN OYEWOLE, "Another Mountain" from *Rooted in the Soil.* Copyright (c) 1993 Abiodun Oyewole.

PUTNAM PUBLISHING GROUP for Bebe Moore Campbell, excerpt from *Sweet Summer.* Copyright (c) 1989 Bebe Moore Campbell.

RANDOM HOUSE for Toni Cade Bambara, "Raymond's Run" from *Gorilla, My Love.* Copyright (c) 1970 Toni Cade Bambara. / Maya Angelou, "On the Pulse of Morning" from *On the Pulse of Morning.* Copyright (c) 1993 Maya Angelou. Reprinted by permission of Random House, Inc.

MARIAN SEARCHINGER ASSOCIATES for Ossie Davis, excerpt from *Escape to Freedom.* Copyright (c) 1976 Ossie Davis.

STERLING LORD LITERISTIC, INC. for Amamu Amiri Baraka, "Ka 'Ba" from *Black Magic (Collected Poetry, 1961–1967).*

ART ACKNOWLEDGMENTS

cover: My Mother's Work, designed by Roland L. Freeman, copyright © 1991 by Roland L. Freeman.

p. 3   Short Stories, Joseph Holston, courtesy of the artist

p. 41   Gemini I, Lev T. Mills, The Evans-Tibbs Collection

p. 87   Two Dancers, Joseph Holston, courtesy of the artist

p. 107 Man with a Horn, Gilbert Fletcher, courtesy of the artist